What people are saying about *What If?*

My dear friend, Pastor Tommy Barnett, has been part of Church Growth International for more than 30 years. He has the gifts of evangelism, encouragement, and faith. He has brought hope to countless people as the Holy Spirit has given him tremendous visions and dreams. Pastors, leaders, and other motivated people need to read *What If?* As you read these pages, you will be amazed by the truth that God can greatly use you—beyond your greatest expectations. God's dream for you will become your dream. God's love for you will saturate your very being. You will see a world full of pain and say to yourself . . . "What if I believed God for more? Always more?"

> Dr. Yonggi Cho
> Senior Pastor Emeritus, Yoido Full Gospel Church
> Seoul, Korea

Tommy Barnett's ministry philosophy has impacted thousands of leaders . . . find a need and fill it; find a hurt and heal it. I am confident that as you read the story of his life, you will be inspired to take your ministry and life to the next level. Thank you, Pastor Tommy, for a life well led and a book well written.

> Doug Clay
> General Superintendent, Assemblies of God USA
> Springfield, Missouri

As a representative of his Lord and Savior Jesus Christ, Tommy Barnett's life is an amazing journey that has impacted hundreds of thousands of people and tens of thousands of pastors. His development of over 300 community ministries, called Dream Centers, is indicative of his heart for the hurting, homeless and addicted in our society. He is true man of God, and his book is a great read as we follow his path.

> Jerry Colangelo
> Partner, JDM Partners, LLC, Phoenix, Arizona
> Former Owner of Phoenix Suns Basketball and Arizona
> Diamondbacks Baseball

Pastor Tommy Barnett is one of the finest leaders of our time. His life of faithfulness and his ministry longevity have impacted millions of people, inspiring them to dream bigger and accomplish more for God's Kingdom. I honor and thank Pastor Tommy Barnett for his imprint in my life and the world.

Pastor Herbert Cooper
Senior Pastor, People's Church
Oklahoma City, Oklahoma

Today, we look at the Dream Centers appearing in cities across the globe, and it's truly incredible to watch God heal the hurting, mend the broken, and feed the hungry. But when I read this book, I realized the amazing things happening today are the fruit of a long life dedicated to the gospel of Christ—a gospel that saves, heals, and restores. That's the gospel we need to share with people in our communities.

Wilfredo "Choco" De Jesús
Senior Pastor, New Life Covenant Church
Chicago, Illinois

I have the unbelievable privilege of leading the college named in honor of Pastor Tommy Barnett. His life exemplifies everything we champion: the Gospel of Jesus Christ is the hope of the world and has the power to change a life and transform a city. *What If?* gives all of us the chance to be inspired by his story once again. In these pages, we'll realize there's always more we can do for Jesus, and He will give us everything we need to see it happen.

Dr. Alan Ehler, D.Min.
Dean, Barnett College of Ministry and Theology,
Southeastern University
Lakeland, Florida

As a young aspiring minister, I first met Pastor Tommy at the Dream Center after a Thursday night service. My brief interaction with him was full of life, encouragement, and caused me to dream bigger. I believe the stories in these pages will do the same for you, because this is who I know Pastor Tommy to be. Reading this book feels like he is sitting with you sharing stories of God's faithfulness, miracles, a commitment to the gospel, and love for "the least of these." Pastor Tommy's life will inspire you to love more and dream bigger!

Pastor Daniel Floyd
Senior Pastor, Lifepoint Church
Fredericksburg, Virginia

Tommy Barnett is one of the most inspirational voices of our time. His passion for reaching lost, hurting, and downtrodden people has motivated a generation of church leaders to make a difference. Learn everything you can about this man—it will make you more like Jesus!

Pastor Willie George
Founding Pastor, Church on the Move
Tulsa, Oklahoma

Among a handful of key people God has used to inspire me, I am blessed to count my friend Tommy Barnett among them. I know I'm not the only one, and now in *What If?* Tommy shares his life story so others can grow closer in their relationship with God as they serve according to His purposes. With wisdom, encouragement, and insight on leadership, Tommy's heart for loving others reveals a contagious example of what it means to follow Jesus. Be warned—don't read *What If?* unless you're prepared to let God answer that question in your own life!

Chris Hodges
Senior Pastor, Church of the Highlands, Author of *The Daniel Dilemma* and *What's Next?*
Birmingham, Alabama

From prisons to palaces, my friend Tommy Barnett has impacted people in all walks of life with the Good News of Jesus Christ. He is a dreamer who, in many years of life and ministry, has surrendered all to the great adventure of living in God's will. I have the highest regard for Tommy, and he has been an incredible inspiration to me personally. I know the story of what God has done in and through his life will embolden you to believe there is always more on the horizon.

Brian Houston
Global Senior Pastor, Hillsong Church
Sydney, Australia

Pastor Tommy Barnett is a modern-day pillar of the faith. No one has embodied a commitment to innovation and empowering the next generation like Pastor Tommy. His life in ministry is a story worth telling as a part of equipping the next generation of leaders so that they can go into the world as influential servants in their careers and their communities. This book tells of a journey that future church leaders need to hear.

Dr. Kent J. Ingle, MTS, D.Min.
President, Southeastern University
Lakeland, Florida

Pastor Tommy Barnett is one of the most innovative, progressive-thinking individuals of his era. His timely autobiography, *What If?*, will be a priceless resource to build faith, avoid stumbling blocks and attain spiritual gratification. I strongly recommend this as a resource to every believer and especially every leader.

T. D. Jakes, Sr.
Senior Pastor, The Potter's House of Dallas, Inc. / TDJ Enterprises
New York Times Best-selling Author

I was 19, struggling with addiction, rejection, and brokenness. I had a hard heart and believed everyone had given up on me . . . until I met the Pastor at the end of a service. I was giving God one last shot when that Pastor took a look at me and said, "I don't know what you've done, but I love you and I want you in my church." That man was Tommy Barnett, and my life was forever changed by God that day!

Aaron Jayne
Senior Pastor, Coastline Church
Carlsbad, California

Today more than ever, we need spiritual fathers to show us how to live, serve, and lead. More than anyone I know, Tommy Barnett has stepped up to be that model for countless pastors like me. From the first day I heard about him years ago to the many times I've had the privilege to interact with him, I've seen his huge heart . . . for Jesus, for the lost, for the hurting, and for pastors who are following God's call. There haven't been many leaders like Tommy, but he has left his imprint on me and many others. This book is the story of his life, but more than that, it points us to the One he has followed so passionately his whole life.

Rob Ketterling
Lead Pastor, River Valley Church
Minneapolis-St.Paul, Minnesota

In his own words, Pastor Tommy Barnett says his autobiography *What If?* "is all about a great and mighty God who is able to use a flawed but willing man to bring glory to the name of Jesus." It's for us to dream, he urges; after that, God makes provision for the vision. And Tommy Barnett has dreamed big: building megachurches with hundreds of community missions, bringing thousands upon thousands of people to Christ, and creating incredible Dream Centers to serve the forgotten and disadvantaged. In our more than three decades of friendship, I've witnessed all of this, and I've never failed to be inspired by his dreams and his heart for helping the lost.

Jon Kyl, former US Senator from Arizona
Phoenix, Arizona

In *What If?*, Tommy Barnett says that his chief regret is that he should have "dreamed bigger dreams and taken bigger risks." I want to tell him, "Are you kidding? You've dreamed bigger dreams than anyone I know, and you've put your life on the line again and again for the sake of Jesus and the Great Commission." Thank you, Tommy, for being the example so many of us have had the opportunity to follow.

Justin Lathrop
Vice President for Strategic Partnerships, Southeastern University
Lakeland, Florida

I can still remember the first time that I heard Pastor Tommy Barnett speak. It was at the Australian National Assemblies of God conference in a jam-packed arena in early 1990. Along with 12,000 others, I was completely mesmerized as he spoke. I had never been so gripped by a man with a message like I was that night. He instantly shot to hero status in my life! Pastor Tommy became the benchmark of what a minister of Christ looked like, and I dearly wanted to follow and emulate him! Pastor Tommy's love for the church, for the lost, for the broken and the hopeless has challenged me and shaped my ministry philosophy over the years. His passion for souls, for creative "out of the box" evangelism, and for equipping leaders has rarely been rivaled, and is reflected in his books and in his sermons. I know I wouldn't be who I am today or where I am today without this extraordinary man's influence in my life. I honestly believe he will go down in history as one of the great church builders and influencers of our lifetime. It's an honor to know him.

Pastor Jurgen Matthesius
Lead Pastor, C3 Church
San Diego, California and Salt Lake City, Utah

I've known Tommy for many years and I've had the privilege of watching God use him in countless ways. His energy is boundless . . . and so is his faith. He has always been willing to take huge risks to see what God might do. Tommy has lived without a safety net. No, that's not true. God has always been there to lead him, empower him, and bless people through him.

John C. Maxwell
Best-selling Author, Speaker and Founder of The John Maxwell Co.

I have a short list of modern-day leaders I want to study more. Now, with this book, generations to come have been given the gift of seeing into the heart and life of one of these great leaders. Tommy Barnett's life story left me speechless.

Marcus Mecum
Senior Pastor, 7 Hills Church
Florence, Kentucky

Tommy Barnett is my Pastor and an amazing man of God. He knows the true meaning of the Gospel of Jesus Christ and has lived it to the fullest. His example has impacted my life personally, helping me pursue God's purpose for believers in Christ to, as he says, "Find a need and fill it . . . find a hurt and heal it." I believe every person who reads *What If?* will become more convinced of God's love and desire to do more than they can ask or imagine in their lives!

Joyce Meyer
Bible Teacher and Best-selling Author

Tommy's passion and enthusiasm for Jesus are contagious and jump off the pages of this book. *What If?* will stir your faith to believe God for more!

Dr. Todd Mullins
Senior Pastor, Christ Fellowship
West Palm Beach, Florida

WOW! I have been hoping for over 25 years that Tommy Barnett would write this book! All of us will grow, be challenged, and feel compelled to do more for the glory of God because of Tommy's life and experiences. I can't think of anyone that has been on the front line of expanding God's Kingdom and growing His church for over 60 years like Tommy Barnett!! Get ready, you are in for a life and ministry changing ride!

Charles Nieman
Senior Pastor, Abundant Living Faith Center
El Paso, Texas

Tommy Barnett is without any doubt one of the greatest voices of our time. It is a voice of a life that gushes passion for Jesus and reaching the lost no matter what it takes. What he has done to awaken the Church to the importance of focusing on the poor and the hurting has inspired me over and over.

Dino Rizzo
Executive Director, ARC (Association of Related Churches)
Associate Pastor, Church of the Highlands
Birmingham, Alabama

Pastor Tommy Barnett is a multi-generational leader who embodies the gospel message by dedicating his life to serving the needs of the outcast, ostracized, and overlooked. His impact and influence have not only changed the trajectory and relevance of the local church; he has also captured the hearts of ordinary people who have been mobilized to live beyond themselves. Pastor Tommy's heart and passion have been fuel to my mission and our church's mission to impact our city and beyond.

Jimmy Rollins
Lead Pastor, i5 City
Baltimore, Maryland

I'm so excited about this amazing book about the life of Pastor Tommy Barnett. It's the story of a man whose faith I've witnessed and esteemed for many years. I've had the privilege of knowing Pastor Tommy since I was a boy and he, not unlike my Dad who was one of his peers and friends, is one of my heroes in how he's lived this adventure of believing God time after time after time. This book is filled with the stories of those "What If?" moments that capture his approach to impossible circumstances and daring to believe God for MORE. I'm so glad his inspiring journey has been chronicled—his life has always inspired me, and now we have it to encourage and enjoy for generations to come.

Judah Smith
Lead Pastor, Churchome
Seattle and Los Angeles

Tommy Barnett is my longtime mentor and close friend, and his story has truly inspired me to dream big, achieve more, and trust God for what seems impossible. Now, in the pages of *What If?* Pastor Tommy shares his incredible, true story with a world longing to believe. As you engage his story, you'll be moved to ask, "What if I dream bigger? What if I trust God more? What if . . .?" Dare to read and discover what's possible when we refuse to put limits on God. Then let *What If?* supercharge your belief in what God can do through *your* story!

Steve Smothermon
Senior Pastor, Legacy Church
Albuquerque, New Mexico

To say that I can't wait for this book to come out is an understatement! Tommy Barnett is one of the most innovative and inspirational leaders of our time. He has inspired many of us to dream bigger dreams and trust God for things previously thought impossible. Do yourself a favor and get the book!

Greg Surratt
President of the Association of Related Churches (ARC)
Founding Pastor, Seacoast Church
Mt. Pleasant, South Carolina

One of the major takeaways from *What If?* is a glimpse of Pastor Tommy Barnett's faith in God through different seasons of his life. Throughout this book, you will see a person whose trust in God fueled his faith for more, and he never gave up on what God was leading him to do. This book isn't merely a collection of stories of one man's life—it's a well of wisdom on how to have faith in God for a lifetime. It is an honor to know Pastor Tommy, a man who has given his life to people all over the world. I have been personally impacted in a profound way from his life and ministry.

Chad Veach
Lead Pastor, Zoe Church
Los Angeles, California

Pastor Tommy Barnett is a living legend! His enduring example of unstoppable faith, hope and love has inspired countless people all over the world to fill needs and heal hurts wherever they may be found. For those of us who think we know the story of Tommy Barnett, let his autobiography be an invitation to learn from and celebrate the life of one of the most consequential Christian leaders on the earth today.

Jonathan Wiggins
Lead Pastor, Rez Church
Loveland, Colorado

After being in full-time ministry for over 50 years, I have become a student of both the past and the present. After watching leaders come and go, it's become obvious that a unique breed of leaders has been able to stand the test of time and separated themselves from the proverbial herd by upholding a set of Biblical principles of evangelism. These leaders have moved men and women to do more for God than they ever thought possible.

Tommy Barnett is one of those leaders. I am very aware that I am a direct result of the power and influence of the principles he has taught and lived. His heart and strategy have become the foundation of what is now Metro World Child, the largest Sunday school in the world, with nearly 250,000 in attendance each week.

Thank you, Pastor Barnett, my friend. You have challenged and inspired many people over your amazing life—especially me. One thing is sure: there is certainly MORE to come.

Bill Wilson
Founder and Senior Pastor, Metro World Child
Brooklyn, New York

Why read this biography of Tommy Barnett? Because it will make you a better follower of Jesus! Because it will enlarge your vision and inspire your faith and passion to do great things for God and for people! Because it communicates authenticity, courage and vulnerability as indispensable ingredients for life and ministry!

Dr. George O. Wood
Chairman, World AG Fellowship
The General Council of the Assemblies of God
Springfield, Missouri

Tommy Barnett

What If?

MY STORY OF BELIEVING GOD FOR MORE
... *ALWAYS* MORE

Foreword by Jentezen Franklin

Jacket and interior design by Anne McLaughlin, Blue Lake Design
Author photos on jacket and page 325 by Meshali Mitchell, meshali.co

ISBN: 978-1-64296-013-6
Published by ARC, The Association of Related Churches
Printed in the United States

Southeastern University is proud to commission this important book. Tommy Barnett is the Chancellor of SEU, and he has been such a powerful influence on the students, faculty, and administration that we have named the College of Ministry & Theology in his honor.

I dedicate this book to the faithful, loyal people who have stood with
me and allowed me to pursue the *what ifs* of life:
My father, Reverend Hershel Barnett, who first engraved
the love of souls on my heart.
My mother, Joy Barnett, who was everything her name signifies.
My wife, Marja, whose unselfish love has given me
the freedom to follow the dream.
My children, Kristie, Luke, and Matthew, who are my source of
constant pleasure and blessing. You have taken the baton, and you're
running faster and farther than me.

This book is the product of many faithful men and women who,
through almost 300 Dream Centers around the world,
extend their *hands* to offer genuine help,
their *feet* to meet people where they are,
and their *hearts* to break with the poor, alcoholics and addicts,
the sick, the lonely, the immigrants, the outcasts,
the victims of human trafficking, and the depressed—
the kind of people who were, more than anyone else,
the recipients of Jesus' compassion.

Table of Contents

Foreword

I am convinced that if a name was added to the eleventh chapter of The Book of Hebrews today, Tommy Barnett would be listed among the most faithful for his era. No one on the planet has done more to be the hands and feet of Jesus to "the least of these" than the ministries he has founded and supported. His heart has no bounds, and he has been to the ends of the earth raising support and being a spiritual father to so many who are striving to reach the lost, feed the hungry, and rescue the perishing from lives of addiction, prostitution, and human trafficking. He is fearless and a national treasure in every sense of the word.

For many years Tommy Barnett has been one of a handful of mentors and spiritual fathers to me. I know our ministry has experienced countless blessings because of our association and support for his many missions and outreaches. I can't think of a better title for a book written by his hand than *What If?* Tommy Barnett is a living example of all that is possible if we will just say those two words: What if? I have no doubt he has said these two words many times in his lifetime and will again. These two words have helped rescue thousands of lives that the rest of society has written off, and the impact of his endeavors has affected the trajectory of countless families while changing the moral fabric of neighborhoods and entire cities.

Many have dreamed amazing dreams, but few have actually braved the obstacles and opposition to rise up and allow the Lord to use them day after day, year after year . . . brick upon brick and life upon life like Tommy Barnett has. His family is a testament to God's faithfulness to the next generation. I challenge you to allow each chapter to speak into YOUR dream . . . your "what if" and to open your mind and heart to all that is possible. Tommy Barnett's life has marked the trail for you on each page in this book. I challenge you to attach his legacy to your calling and his anointing to your vision, and then, allow his passion to start an unquenchable fire in your belly.

Jentezen Franklin
Senior Pastor, Free Chapel
Gainesville, Georgia

FESTIVAL OF LIFE, BANGALORE, INDIA

Find a Need and Fill It

*A*s I stood on a high platform in Bangalore, India, I looked over a sea of humanity like nothing I'd ever seen before. As far as I could see, the crowd of over 400,000 people extended into the night. They had come to hear the gospel of Jesus.

Ten years earlier, Joyce Meyer had asked me to be her pastor. When she scheduled her crusade in Bangalore, she invited me to join her and her husband Dave, and she gave me the honor of speaking on one of the nights.

As I stood next to her on the platform, my mind drifted back to my uncle Ted Vassar, who as a young man 100 years before had come to India with his wife to build an orphanage in Pune, a city in the western part of the country. When I was a boy, I loved to hear him tell stories of his adventures in his adopted country. He talked about a boy who had been attacked by a leopard. Uncle Ted heard the screams, grabbed his rifle, and ran to help. The leopard had the boy's leg in its mouth when Uncle Ted shot and killed it. The doctors looked at the mangled leg and planned to amputate, but Uncle Ted and others prayed all night before the operation, and by the next morning, the leg was better and was saved. The boy saw this miracle from God, and his faith was enflamed. He grew up to lead a great revival in Nagaland, India.

My uncle's years at the orphanage were full of joy and tragedy. They reached many children living in poverty and on the streets. On some mornings, he found children who had been left on the doorstep overnight. But two of his own children were buried there. One died in childbirth and the other at thirteen with a ruptured appendix. Both could have been saved if they'd had proper medical attention, but there were no hospitals in the area.

On the platform that night in Bangalore, I turned to Joyce and told her about my missionary uncle who, 100 years earlier, had sown seeds of the gospel that we were joyfully reaping. I said, "Joyce, I wish my Uncle Ted could see this sight. I'm sure he couldn't have fathomed this kind of harvest!"

That night, I preached with a blend of passion and joy. At the end, tens of thousands of people raised their hands to indicate they had trusted in Jesus.

I wasn't alone on my trip to Bangalore. Dino Rizzo was with me. During the day, Dino and I taught 20,000 pastors how to follow up with those who had trusted Christ and grow their churches. As I always do when I travel to cities around the world, I opened the window of my hotel room and looked over the sprawling city. I scanned the new office buildings and the slums, the parks and the streets packed with people—mostly people who didn't know Jesus. In every city, I imagine what it would mean to those people to have a gospel-preaching church that cares for their needs.

One night, Dino and I stayed up long past midnight talking about God's heart for the disadvantaged . . . in Bangalore and in the cities of America where we served. Dino knew my heart is always for the lost to come to faith, but both of us sensed that God wanted us to provide resources—tangible, specific resources that could save or change lives—for people who were overlooked by society. We looked at passages of Scripture, imagined what God might do through our churches, and encouraged each other to "excel still more." It was a wonderful conversation, one I'll always remember. It wouldn't be our last.

At the time, the Dream Center was just taking shape in Phoenix. We were taking our first steps to create permanent structures that would be a lifeline to the poor, alcoholics and addicts, the sick, the lonely, the immigrants, the outcasts, the victims of human trafficking, and the depressed—the kind of people who were, more than anyone else, the recipients of Jesus' compassion.

Throughout my life, I've sensed God's clear call to find a need and fill it, to find a hurt and heal it. Do people need the life-changing message of the gospel of grace? More than anything else. Do they need to see God's people, His body, extend their hands to offer genuine help, their feet to meet them where they are, and their hearts to break with theirs? In many cases, receiving tangible expressions of love is the only way they will open their hearts to the message of Jesus.

Now, as I near the end of my ministry journey, I look back at the incredible things God has done, and I'm deeply grateful. I've only pastored two churches, but as I've preached in cities all over the world, God has consistently impressed me with the dream that I'd one day start a church there. These churches, He assured me, would reach the people I've always been able to reach: the ones nobody else wanted.

Has God fulfilled this vision? Yes, in a big way!

Early in my ministry, I felt called to begin a Pastors & Leaders School. Nothing fancy. I just invited a bunch of pastors to come, and I shared the things that worked for me in reaching out into the community. I explained that little things matter, like my conviction that the altar call begins in the parking lot before the church service even starts, running a bus ministry because if you get kids in church their parents will follow, and encouraging people to follow their dreams for their own ministry, even if I didn't think they had a chance at succeeding. But most important, I told the pastors how to get people saved and keep them in church. Over the years, we've had 250,000 pastors come through our Pastors & Leaders School. I remember a lot of these events, but one stands out and has special meaning for me.

I had been serving as the Senior Pastor of what used to be called Phoenix First Assembly but is now called the Dream City Church. One year, about 7,000 pastors showed up from all over the world to attend our Pastors & Leaders School. The place was packed, and all the pastors were really fired up. Even before the service started, they yelled chants much like they do at college basketball games. Pastors on one side of the church began shouting, "We love Jesus, yes we do! We love Jesus, how about you?" Then the pastors on the other side of the church answered back just as loudly, "We love Jesus, yes we do! We love Jesus how about you?" The air was filled with excitement. Actually, whenever we have a Pastors & Leaders School, it's always the same response. People come expecting big things to happen.

At this particular event, I had invited the marching band from the biggest high school in town to march into the church with the drum-line beating out a stirring song before fanning out on the platform to play our national anthem. Imagine 7,000 pastors singing "The Star-Spangled Banner" at the top of their lungs. It was pretty amazing, and what God was going to do was only just beginning.

I calmed them down long enough to begin with a prayer and a few words of welcome, and then I announced that we would begin with a "parade of ministry" to give them a glimpse into what we do in our church to reach people, but more importantly, to cast a vision for the kinds of things they could do when they got back to their churches. I believe that no matter who you are, how much money you have or don't have, whether you are young or old, there's a place for you to serve in church. We were blessed to have 265 unique ministries in ours, and they were about to stride across the platform as our 300-voice choir and full orchestra began playing the hymns and rousing choruses of the church.

First, our special-needs kids literally danced across the stage—kids with Down syndrome and other challenges—waving and so proud to be recognized. We gave them candy to throw out to the pastors, and I don't know who was happier, the kids or the pastors.

Then the audit committee marched across the stage, and you guessed it—they threw some dollar bills out into the crowd, and I *know* the pastors loved that! Then it was our wheelchair ministry's turn. Fifty of our members in their wheelchairs were pushed by the

THE PARADE OF MINISTRIES

volunteers who helped get them to church every Sunday and cared for their needs during the week. One of them carried a big sign: "The Holy Rollers Welcome You!" If you've ever wondered if it's possible to laugh and cry at the same time, these cheering pastors would settle that question once and for all.

The next ministry literally roared onto the platform—our motorcycle church. Can you imagine a dozen Harleys ridden by guys wearing leather jackets and chaps inside a church? What better place for them, right? Most have been saved from the wild and dangerous world of motorcycle gangs. We love seeing them grow in their love for Jesus—a love that compels them to reach out to people only they could reach: motorcycle gang members.

You might wonder how we are able to get motorcycles inside the church and onto the stage. You can thank the elephants. I'd better explain that one. You see, I believe that whatever the church does, they should do it to the glory of God. One of the ways we serve our community is by presenting professional-level musical events that sell out faster than a Broadway hit. To do that, we needed to design our building to accommodate whatever it takes to provide such world-class entertainment, and often those pageants include live animals . . . including elephants. If we can get an elephant on the platform, a Harley is a piece of cake.

Throughout the years, I've heard people say disparagingly, "Barnett's only interested in numbers." They mean it as criticism, but I take it as a compliment because every number represents a soul that Jesus loves and gave His life for so they could be saved. I'll do just about anything in good taste to let people know that God loves them and gave His Son for them. That's why we have 265 ministries in our church. It's not only about introducing them to Jesus. We want everyone to get involved in the life of the church, to grow and develop a passion for winning others to Christ. If one of our 265 ministries isn't the right fit for someone, we'll add another one.

After the smoke cleared from the motorcycles, our deaf ministry paraded past the cheering pastors. Then, ministry by ministry, ordinary people who serve or benefit proudly marched to the cheers and applause of those 7,000 pastors: senior adults, alcohol recovery, faith and fitness, foster care, meals for the homeless, bus ministry—and on and on until we came to our last ministry, the drama department. And suddenly, there was with the multitudes, angels descending from the ceiling! Horses, lambs, cows, tigers, and yes, the elephant and all their handlers filled the platform with wonder, and by then the pastors were openly weeping. That's when it hit me.

God was doing exactly what He said He would do. Every time I visited a city and looked out over its streets, watched its people, and felt the emptiness of its lost, I clearly heard God tell me I would start a church there and thousands of souls would invite Jesus into their hearts. Up until now, I had only two churches to show Him. But as I watched this group of sold-out pastors weep at the potential their churches represented, I realized God's promise was happening right before my very eyes. Each one of these pastors—and thousands before them who had come to our school—were doing what I couldn't possibly do. In His great wisdom and providence, God knew why He planted the seed in my heart for my Pastors & Leaders School.

This impact has been one of the greatest blessings of my life, and to be honest, a big surprise. Over many decades, God has used me in ways I could never have imagined when I started. Through it all, I've tried to be a tool in the hands of God. Availability is the first step toward usefulness.

Do you ever wonder what He wants to do through you?

Of course, you do. That's why I'm writing this book. If God can use a skinny little kid from the oil fields of Texas to build His kingdom, He can certainly use you. I would be nothing without the influence of great godly men and women who have poured so much wisdom into

AT THE PHOENIX PASTORS & LEADERS SCHOOL

me and the power of the Holy Spirit who has enabled me to do things way beyond my wildest dreams.

One thing is for sure: Until the Lord returns, we'll never run out of needs to fill and hurts to heal. The question isn't one of *their need* but of *our care*. Where does compassion come from? We love because we've experienced the tender love of Jesus, we forgive because we're amazed that He has cleansed us from all sin by His sacrifice on the cross, and we accept those who aren't like us because God in Christ accepted us when we were nothing like Him. In everything we do, we go back to the cross of Jesus.

Throughout my life, God has continually prodded and prompted me to ask, "What if?"

What if I started preaching? Would anyone come to hear me? Would God use me to touch people's hearts with the gospel?

What if I buy a huge tent? Will it be empty, or will God fill it?

What if I answer God's call to a small church in Iowa? Will God bless us there?

What if I buy a fleet of buses and bring people from miles away to worship with us? Will people come or will those buses become monuments to a failed dream?

What if I go to a church where I really don't want to go? Can that possibly be His leading?

What if we build a huge building? Will people come, or will there be only echoes?

What if God tells me I'll pastor a historic church in Los Angeles?

What if God puts it on our hearts to create a place where people who have lost hope can renew their dreams?

What if God multiplies those places of healing all over the world?

What if the recurring impression to plant churches in every city where I travel is fulfilled by training hundreds of thousands of pastors to experience God's power and blessing in ministry?

What if we take bold steps through the door of opportunity that God opens in front of us?

Through all these years, "What if?" has been quickly followed by "Why not?" and then "Wow! God is doing amazing things."

This book contains my story, but as you'll see, it's much more than that. It's actually God's story of moving in the hearts and minds of people in our city, across our country, and around the world. Throughout my life, God has given me a clear sense of purpose. He has continually inspired me to dream bigger, reach higher, and trust Him for far more that I could imagine. On every page, I hope you recognize the amazing love in God's heart and His kindness to use someone like me to tell people about the grace I've found—and they can find—in Jesus Christ.

Love for Tommy Joe

13 MONTHS OLD WITH MOTHER

CHAPTER 1

Genesis

y grandfather, Tom Barnett, moved to Electra, Texas, in 1937 with his wife Ruth, their son Hershel, and three daughters so he could work in the oil fields. The town is near the Red River in north Texas, just west of Wichita Falls. It was named for the daughter of a man who owned the Waggoner Ranch, the second largest in the state. The area suffers from severe droughts, and when the town was founded in the 19th century, the water at the bottom of the wells was contaminated by a foul substance. Years later, drillers tapped into that substance in one of the biggest oil discoveries in the history of Texas. They called it "the Clayco gusher."

Like all oil booms, this one attracted a crowd eager for work, especially during the dark days of the Depression. My grandfather and his family leased a small house next to a pump house owned by the Magnolia Oil Company, his new employer. Hershel, my dad, was a traveling evangelist, which wasn't exactly the best paying job during that time. Churches had difficulty paying their light bills, so they had very little to pay an evangelist. Hershel and his wife Joy saved money by living with his parents next to the pump house.

From the stories I've heard, God certainly had his hand on Hershel. Often, the Holy Spirit moved so powerfully that churches asked him to stay and preach another week, and sometimes a third. People kept showing up and trusting in Jesus, and nobody wanted it to end. On a few occasions, over half of the people in a town came forward during a revival. The sight of these people at the altar meant far more to Hershel than all the money in the world.

When Joy told him she was pregnant, Hershel was thrilled! He hoped he would be the kind of father his dad had been for him. On a cold October evening in 1937, Hershel and his dad were sitting in the living room reading the Bible when my grandmother called out, "I think it's time! Joy is going into labor. Hershel, call Dr. Davis!"

Hershel jumped up, but my grandfather beat him to the phone. He gave a few turns to the crank to get the operator's attention, and then he almost shouted, "Sally, this is Tom Barnett next to the pump house on the Waggoner Ranch. Our son's wife is going into labor, and we need Dr. Davis!"

The operator immediately called the doctor and asked him to go to Tom's house as fast as he could drive. The lights of Electra could be seen from the house, but it was ten miles away on a narrow dirt road. It took the doctor an excruciatingly long time to get there, but finally, the car stopped in front of the house. Dr. Davis grabbed his black bag and ran inside.

It was a long and difficult labor. Hershel was distraught when he heard Joy's screams of pain, so Tom took him outside to sit on the porch. Finally, my grandmother stepped to the front door and smiled, "It's a boy!"

Hershel ran back into the house just as Dr. Davis was washing his hands and packing his bag. Hershel stopped for a moment to thank him, and then he tiptoed into the bedroom. He looked at Joy and his newborn baby. He knelt beside her, kissed her cheek, and stared for the first time into the face of his son.

He turned to Joy and whispered, "I love you so much. He's really something, isn't he?" He paused for a second and then told her, "And so are you!"

Joy asked, "Do you want to hold him?"

He gently picked up the little boy and held him to his chest for a long time. Then he said to Joy, "I'd like to name him after my dad, Tom." Joy was delighted.

From the moment of my birth, my parents and grandparents had a special sense that God was going to use me to accomplish purposes far beyond anything they could imagine. I don't often tell this part of the story because it sounds so strange to modern ears, but in the time when I was born (which seems to many like it was before Abraham came on the scene!), this concept was widely accepted. Let me explain. Ruth, my grandmother, insisted that I was born with a veil covering my face. She also claimed that when this happens, it's a sign of special destiny—the child will someday do great things. Was she exaggerating or confused after all the stress and excitement? Apparently not. According to medical sources, what appears to be a veil is actually a piece of membrane known as a *caul.*

I believe in the supernatural—God can do absolutely anything He wants to do through anyone He chooses. He can make Abraham a father when he was 100 years old, He can spare three Hebrew boys from Nebuchadnezzar's fiery furnace, He can save the world through a Son born to a virgin, and He can use a person born next to a pump house in an oil field to reach the lost and care for people in need. I'm living proof of the amazing kindness, wisdom, and power of God.

A caul occurs rarely . . . about once in every 80,000 births. Whether it's merely folklore or divine providence, I'm not sure, but I know one thing: God has taken me from that little pump house in

7 MONTHS OLD WITH DAD

Electra to places I never dreamed I'd go, and for only one purpose—
to find a need and fill it, to find a hurt and heal it.

In the spring of 1939, when I was about eighteen months old, my
dad was on the road again. He was preaching a revival at a church in
Granite City, Illinois. As it often happened, God did so much in the
first week that the church asked him to stay for two more weeks. He
was really excited to see God move in so many lives.

One day during the third week, my mother called the pastor in
Granite City and asked to speak to my dad. He found my dad and
gave him the phone. Her voice was urgent and trembling: "Hershel,
you need to come home. Tommy's really sick! The doctor said it's
pneumonia, and he may die!"

In those days, there was no effective treatment for pneumonia.
Penicillin had been discovered in 1928, but it wasn't used to treat

patients before World War II. A diagnosis of pneumonia, especially in a child, was very serious.

When Dad got off the phone, he got on his knees and prayed, "God, I want to go home, but You're blessing this revival. Please tell me what to do!"

The Lord spoke clearly to him, "If you'll put My work first, I'll take care of your work."

Heartbroken, my dad called back home to let Mom know that the Lord had spoken to his heart, and he had to continue with the revival. It would be several days before he came home. When my grandmother heard that Dad wasn't coming home, she got on the phone to give her son an earful! "Son, you get home right now! You're terrible. You're hardhearted. Get back here and take care of your wife and son!"

In spite of his mom's insistence, Dad knew he had to obey God. He continued preaching every night, trusting God to keep His word. But each day he got another phone call telling him my condition was getting worse. With faith and determination, Dad preached until the final night of the revival, and every night more and more people accepted Christ.

As soon as he finished preaching on the last night, he ran to his car and drove all night to get back to Electra. As his old car rumbled down the final miles of the dirt road leading to his parents' house, the country doctor's car approached from the opposite direction. As the two cars passed, the doctor looked over at my dad and shrugged his shoulders.

"Oh no," my dad thought. "I'm too late!"

He raced the last mile and a half, jumped out of the car, and ran into the house. The first thing he saw was his little boy happily crawling across the floor. He learned from my mom that on the final night of the revival, my condition markedly improved, and by that morning I was crawling around and getting into things like any other toddler.

My father was deeply devoted to his family. As you'll see in the rest of my story, he played an enormously positive role in my life. He was, and still is, the finest example of a father, husband, and leader I've ever known. Throughout his years in ministry, my dad found ways to balance his commitment to God and his commitment to us. He put God and his family first, and the people he served came next. There were times when God directed Dad to serve Him when it was inconvenient and he was misunderstood. In these moments, God was testing Dad to see if he would put Him first. That's what happened when I was sick and God told Dad to stay at the revival instead of coming home. My dad obeyed God even though it didn't make sense to Mom and his parents, and God honored his obedience. When he got home, instead of finding a very sick child, or maybe a dead child, he saw me crawling around, happy and full of life.

I believe God wants us to be completely sold out to Him—no reservations and no retreat—but He has also called us to be dedicated, loving, attentive spouses and parents. One of the most important things we can do for our families is involve them in our ministries. The Bible says the only way we can minister to God is to minister to people. When we reach out to the poor, the homeless, and the hurting, we're really ministering to God. That's what I've taught my kids. They knew there may be some times when I'd have to change our family's plans because of an emergency or important church business, and I have always tried to make it up to them when that happens. They never resented that.

In January of 1940, Dad held a revival in Kansas City, Kansas. It was so successful that the elders of the church that sponsored the revival asked him to be their pastor. He agreed, so we packed up what little we had, said goodbye to my grandparents, and headed off to what seemed to me to be the biggest city in the world. The church was small—less than a hundred showed up on a good Sunday—and the building was in pretty bad shape. The floor creaked, and wires hung down from the ceiling with bare light bulbs attached—those were our chandeliers. The parsonage was even smaller, but that was fine with us because it was our first house. My mom did her best to turn it into a loving home.

One day when I was four years old, my parents and I got in the car and drove downtown in Kansas City for them to do some shopping. As we drove into the shopping district, I felt a heavy weight on my small shoulders, and it kept getting heavier and heavier. It felt like a ton of weight—literally the weight of the world—was pushing down on me. I was sitting between my mom and dad, and as my dad drove the car, I turned to my mom and asked, "When was I saved?"

"Why Tommy," Mom answered with a surprised look on her face. "You've always been saved."

My dad was a real hellfire and brimstone preacher who regularly warned people to be ready for the second coming of Christ, and at that moment I was afraid that if the Lord returned, I'd be left behind.

"But aren't you supposed to go to the altar and ask Jesus to come into your heart in order to be saved?" I asked.

"Yes, son," Dad answered. "But you don't need to worry. You're already saved."

That must not have been enough for me, so I pressed on. "But when? When was I actually saved?"

They didn't have an answer, which only added to my fears of missing out if Jesus returned before we got back home. I pleaded, "I want to be saved. Right now!"

I must have worn them down because my dad pulled over to the side of the road, and in the car in downtown Kansas City, I knelt between my parents and asked Jesus to come into my life. I'll never forget how the weight was suddenly lifted. I was being raised in a godly home by Christian parents who taught me all about God, and as a little four-year-old boy, I knew I needed to accept Jesus as my Savior.

Even then, I was convinced that God wanted everyone to invite His Son into their lives. I remember many times when my dad gave an altar call, he'd shout out to one of the deacons, "Shut the doors, Bill. Nobody's leaving until I finish the altar call!" And then we'd sing six verses of "Just as I Am" and wait for that last soul to come forward.[1] Finally, he would say, "We're going to sing one more verse, and if no one comes forward we'll close the service." I had such a passion to see people find the Lord that when I heard him say this was the last verse, I sometimes sneaked down to the altar so they'd keep singing and give at least one more person a chance to come forward and receive Jesus as their Savior. I didn't want that altar call to end.

Salvation was important to me because I'd heard my parents stress the need for it so often. They impressed upon me the value of every person's soul. I wanted to make sure mine was saved, and that others would have the opportunity to experience Jesus' saving grace.

---

1   I've realized many young pastors aren't familiar with this powerful song, so I've included it in the appendix. Read it, sing it, and use it to invite people to trust in Jesus.

MY PARENTS

CHRISTMAS PICTURE WITH DAD, MOTHER, AND SISTER VICKIE

Faith and Reason

*I*n our family's move from Electra to Kansas City, my identity changed from an evangelist's kid to a preacher's kid. The distinction, however, didn't make much of a difference to other people. I didn't realize it at the time, but both labels raised a lot of eyebrows because many people assumed that children who grew up in these homes were hardwired to be wild and irresponsible. I beg to disagree. In fact, I can't think of a better way to grow up. I had the opportunity to see what it took to be a great preacher, and from as far back as I can remember, that's all I ever wanted to be.

That's not to say I was always an angel. When I was about ten years old, a good friend and I were excited about trick-or-treating on Halloween. It was, and still is, the best way to get free candy. That year Halloween fell on a Wednesday, and we were planning to go trick-or-treating after church. On the dresser in my bedroom, I had put a jack-o-lantern with a lit candle inside. As we headed out the door to go to church, my buddy asked, "Aren't you going to blow out the candle?"

"Oh yeah. Thanks," I answered as we were about to leave.

I ran back into my room to blow the candle out, but to this day, I honestly can't remember if I blew it out.

When we arrived at church, we settled into our seats, but both of us were thinking far more about the coming adventure of trick-or-treating than the message that night. About halfway through the service, I heard something that made the hair stand up on the back of my neck: the sirens of a fire engine! While my dad was preaching, someone ran into the room and yelled, "The parsonage is on fire!"

Everyone in the congregation rushed out of the church and over to the parsonage. By the time we got there, flames were shooting out of the windows and thick black smoke poured from the roof. Our neighbors gathered around us as we watched the firefighters battle the blaze. Soon, it was clear that the house was gone. Though no one— well, almost no one—knew about the jack-o-lantern on my dresser, I felt as if every eye was on me.

As everyone watched the firemen, my friend betrayed me. In a stage whisper loud enough for people on the edge of the crowd to hear, he blurted out, "I told Tommy to blow the candle out!"

I could have killed that kid on the spot!

After they put the fire out and the embers cooled down, the fire inspector combed through the ashes to determine the cause of the fire. I prayed like I'd never prayed before: "Please, God, don't let him find anything left of that jack-o-lantern on the dresser!"

The next day the inspector came to the church to give his report on how the fire had started. I tagged along with my dad, and we joined the deacons in the church office. The inspector told us, "It could have started in the boy's room, or it could have been caused by faulty wiring."

After listening to the report, the head deacon spoke up. "I'm sure it was the wiring. The electrician warned us that it wasn't any good."

I have never loved deacons as much as I loved them that day!

That line makes for a good joke when I speak to deacons, but in all honesty, I believe it shaped my respect for deacon boards. I've always loved them as friends, and I've never seen them as enemies. In countless experiences, I've learned that if I approach deacons as my allies who want to help me succeed, all the conversations, even the disagreements, go much more smoothly . . . and they might just save my skin, like the deacon did for me when the parsonage burned down.

Growing up a preacher's kid had some other advantages. After serving a few years in Kansas City, my dad was asked to pastor a church in Abilene, Texas. In Texas, football is almost a religion, but not for the people in our church. It was considered an abomination on the order of dancing and playing cards. Our church absolutely forbade its members from going to football games.

Unfortunately—or fortunately for me—my dad loved football, but he didn't dare break the church rules by going to football games at nearby Abilene Christian University. Enough time has passed, however, for me to share a little secret between Dad and me. On Saturdays in the fall, we got up very early and drove about three hours to Ft. Worth to the campus of Texas Christian University (TCU) to watch the Horned Frogs play football. Once we even drove six hours to Houston to watch the TCU play Rice University in the pouring rain. To this day, TCU is my favorite team, and I follow them every year.

I'll never forget the first time we made one of our secret journeys. My dad must have been concerned that I might be learning the wrong lesson because he tried to explain why it wasn't a sin to go to the games. He told me, "Son, that's a stupid rule. Football's not a sin. And we're not being hypocrites because I don't believe what we're doing is wrong. I just don't want to be a stumbling block to the people at the church, so let's just keep this between us."

I loved Dad for not giving in to unreasonable religious rules. I also loved football, and I didn't understand how it could be a sin. He chose to be honest with me, even if it meant being a little sneaky. In the long run, it elevated my respect for him as a man of God who focused on what's important instead of what's insignificant. Those long trips to football games provided great times of bonding with my dad.

On another occasion when we returned to our church in Kansas City, a theater was showing *The Ten Commandments*. That church, like the one in Abilene, considered going to the movies to be sinful. Dad encouraged me to see it, but he explained that he wasn't going with me. "I really want you to see this movie, Tommy, but I can't go with you. If I get caught in a movie theater, the church will run me out of town on a rail."

Dad drove me downtown to the theater and dropped me off. A few hours later when he picked me up, he wanted to know all about it. It was a great movie, and it moved me to see Moses leading the Israelites in living color. I was sad that my dad couldn't see it, but it made me love him even more that he would do things like that for me. He didn't want me to miss a thing.

My parents were very conservative, but they were ahead of their time. For example, when I was a teenager and rock music was all the rage, my dad told me, "I'm not going to tell you that you can't listen to rock music because I know that you can always sneak out and do it—or any other kind of music."

I couldn't believe what I was hearing, but then he continued, "Son, let me also tell you this. Many of the people who play that kind of music use drugs, they use awful language in their songs, and often mock Christianity. Do you think we ought to honor those kind of people?"

That settled it for me. I loved him for reasoning with me and not laying down the law and telling me I couldn't listen to it.

made his point: I never listened to rock because my dad explained his position and left the choice up to me.

Dad taught me a valuable lesson that I applied as I raised my two sons and my daughter: My dad loved me in a way that made it easy to love him. He was consistent, honest, kind, and flexible. He always explained the *why* behind every *what*, and he avoided laying down the law too often or too rigidly, especially when I was a teenager.

I've tried to follow my dad's example. It seems to me that if our kids experience firsthand what we believe about the grace and holiness of God, and we are honest and open with them about it, there is a better chance that they, too, will love God.

MY GRANDFATHER'S RANCH HOUSE
IN ELECTRA, TEXAS

CHAPTER 3

Rattlesnakes and Watermelons

*W*hen I was ten years old and we lived in Kansas City, my parents told me to pack my bags for a special trip: I would be traveling by train to visit my grandparents in Electra, Texas, and I was going by myself. I couldn't have been happier to hear the news. I loved my parents, and I loved listening to my dad preach. For me life in a parsonage was about as good as it gets, but when they told me I'd be spending the summer with my grandparents, I was thrilled. I'd heard so many of my dad's stories about life on the Texas prairie that I couldn't wait to get down there.

On the big day, I was up before dawn and quickly dressed in my best Sunday clothes. I was so excited I could hardly eat the big breakfast my mom had made for me.

"Put this in your pocket," my dad said as he handed me five dollars. "Use it to buy your lunch."

The minutes seemed like hours, but finally, it was time to go. I grabbed my little suitcase, and the three of us drove to the train station. On the way, I'm sure my mom and dad rattled off some important last-minute advice, but I was too excited to listen. I just stared out the window looking for Union Station in the center of downtown Kansas City.

Dad dropped Mom and me off at the curb in front of the enormous revolving glass doors at the entrance to the terminal. He told us to wait while he found a place to park. In what seemed like hours, he came up the sidewalk and took my hand as we pushed through the doors. Instantly, I was in a dream world. The magnificent main hall had a ninety-five-foot ceiling and polished marble floors. It was, I learned later, the second-largest train station in the country. Dad found the ticket window for the Missouri-Kansas-Texas Railroad, gave the agent a few dollars, and then handed me the ticket to an adventure!

Dad looked up at the six-foot diameter clock in the grand hall. It was almost time for departure, so he led us to Platform 3. The bustle of passengers, conductors, and baggage handlers gave me momentary pause. I was barely ten years old, and in a few moments I would be boarding a train for an eight-hour journey to a place I'd never been. And I was, it was now painfully obvious, alone.

Dad saw that I was a little anxious, and he had a plan. We walked along the platform as he looked for a car with empty seats. He turned to me and announced, "Here's one that looks just right for you, Tommy." He approached the conductor, pointed back to me, and told him, "Make sure he gets off at Bowie."

After a couple of hugs, I climbed the stairs into the railcar. The conductor helped me lift my suitcase to the overhead rack, and I settled into the worn leather seat so big it felt like my own personal throne. As the train began to move, I waved at my parents. Finally, I was off to a summer adventure!

When it was time for lunch, I walked to the dining car and entered a world I never knew existed. Crisp linen tablecloths adorned the tables. Bright, shiny silverware flanked large china plates topped with crystal goblets. Waiters in starched white jackets with linen towels draped over one arm came by with silver pitchers to pour glasses of water. One of them motioned for me to have a seat at a table next to a window. I ordered a chicken dinner—and I even got change back from the five-dollar bill my dad had given me.

The changing landscape sped by that afternoon, and I imagined all the fun I would have. As the sun began to dip toward the horizon, the conductor tapped me on the shoulder. "The next stop is Bowie, son." He reached up for my suitcase and smiled as he handed it to me. The train slowed and stopped.

I was wrestling my bag down the steps to the platform when I heard my name. My grandpa and grandma hugged me and told me they were so glad to see me. Within minutes we were heading northwest on U.S. 287, using the hour-and-a-half ride to get reacquainted. By the time the old Chevy pulled into their dusty driveway, I knew I was in for three months of Wild West adventures.

As we walked through the front door, my grandpa casually told me, "First thing in the morning, we need to saddle up a couple of horses and go looking for my mare." He explained how his mare had produced a number of prize-winning racehorses, but she got away one night. But she didn't really get away . . . she had eloped. My grandpa told the story: He had tied his mare to a hitching post as he walked into the house for a drink of water. A stallion from a herd of wild horses that roamed the prairie had his eye on that irresistible beauty of a mare and waited for the right opportunity. While grandpa was

MY GRANDPARENTS OBSERVING
MY FIRST HORSE RIDE, 1939

inside, the stallion came onto the ranch, sneaked up to the house, and chewed through the mare's leather lead. Once she was free, my grandpa's mare apparently couldn't resist the stallion's charm and followed him onto the prairie.

All night, I envisioned two cowboys, fifty years apart in age, galloping off to rescue the stolen mare. That was my introduction to life on the ranch. Welcome to Texas, Tommy!

Every kid should experience at least one summer like the ones I enjoyed on the ranch in Electra. Many mornings after breakfast, my grandma gave me a piece of raw bacon, and I walked to one of the ponds to catch crawdads. Late in the afternoon after my grandpa finished his work, we used the crawdads for bait. We often caught catfish that we cleaned and ate for dinner.

One of my favorite things to do was to make traps to catch possums, raccoons, and even some snakes. In fact, my grandpa used a long stick with a nail driven into the end to hunt rattlesnakes. I can still see those big diamondbacks hanging limp on the end of the stick. They were a real menace, especially to a boy tromping around the gullies out behind the house, so he killed as many as he could find.

I also got my first taste of fund-raising during those summers in Texas, a skill I've put to use many times in my ministry. My grandpa had another plot of land near Bowie where he raised watermelons that grew to be so big I could hardly pick them up. One of my cousins lived nearby, and my grandpa let us sell some of the watermelons alongside the road. He hauled a couple of dozen in his truck, and we found a nice spot to unload them and put up our handmade sign: "Watermelons—50 cents!"

People who stopped were always amazed at the size of our watermelons. After a few hours, we sold all the big watermelons, and all we had left were a few of the smaller ones. My cousin was a few years older than me and knew enough to keep quiet when we were about to make a sale. But I wanted to please the customer, so I jumped right in with my sales pitch: "You think these are something? You should have seen the ones we had earlier! If you come back tomorrow, we'll have more big ones we can sell you."

My cousin wasn't too happy with my approach. After the car drove away without buying a watermelon, he growled, "How are we going to sell the rest of these watermelons if you talk people out of buying them? You're killing our sales!"

I just wanted people to get their money's worth, and that's how I feel when I raise money for the Lord's work. If I can show them how their money will be used to lead people to Christ or meet the needs of hurting people, I feel confident to ask them for money. It's all about being honest—instead of getting as much money out of people as you can.

A few times during the months in Electra, my grandpa took me to visit an uncle who owned a 6,000-acre ranch nearby, and these experiences opened up a whole new world for me. I learned to herd cattle on horseback, bale hay, and even drive a tractor, because on ranches, you didn't need a driver's license to drive farm machinery. My uncle also planted cotton, so I learned to chop cotton, which is walking down the endless rows chopping away at the weeds with a hoe. When the crop was ready, I helped pick it. This was before the days of automated harvesting machines, so it was backbreaking labor out in the hot sun.

Unlike my grandpa, my uncle still had a little of the devil in him. At least that's what I thought whenever he and his ranch hands decided to get a laugh at my expense . . . which was often. One night he took me out in the middle of a field, gave me a bag, and told me, "Tommy, watch for snipes. When you see one, grab it and put it in the bag." He left me out there by myself as he headed back to laugh about it with his buddies. How was I to know the "snipe hunt" was a favorite trick to play on young greenhorns from the city like me.

My uncle also felt it was his duty to make a man out of me, so he regularly put me in a pen of cattle and told me to herd them into the loading chute. Sometimes, one of those big steers put its head down and charged at me, and I raced to jump over the fence. My uncle hated it when I backed down from those steers, and he let me have it, often throwing in a few curse words to make his point.

If that wasn't enough to turn me into a man, he put me up on a big bronco and told one of his ranch hands to give it a poke so it would start bucking. Of course, those horses made quick work of me, sending me flying into a face full of Texas dirt . . . and other stuff. Determined to toughen me up, my uncle made me get back on the horse, but I was soon bucked off again. (To this day, I'm a bit afraid of horses, so his plan backfired.)

Those summers on the ranch were some of the greatest days of my life. I never asked my parents why they sent me there, but I'm pretty sure they thought it would be good for me to get out of the city and have some adventures with my grandparents and my uncle. The summer visits kept me occupied instead of being bored in the city. It was far better to be in the corral or out on the ranch with a cursing uncle than get into trouble in Kansas City during the formative years of adolescence.

Something else happened around this time that changed me forever.

SHIRTLESS AND CARE-FREE AT 13

CHAPTER 4

Midnight Encounter

O ne of the advantages of growing up in a preacher's home is the exposure to my dad's tireless work as a pastor, and also, to the many notable preachers and evangelists who put Victoria Tabernacle—my dad's church—on their itineraries. One of the largest churches in the United States at the time, Victoria Tabernacle drew some of the best preachers in the world, and I loved listening to them.

One of those preachers who held a revival at our church was Ralph Wilkerson. Some might remember him as the founder of Melodyland Christian Center, for several decades one of the largest and most influential churches in the country. Before Wilkerson turned it into a church, Melodyland was a popular 3,200-seat musical theater attracting the great performers of the 1960s, including The Dave Clark Five, Bobby Darin, James Brown, the Grateful Dead, and Connie Stevens. Just down Harbor Boulevard from Disneyland in Anaheim, California, Melodyland became known as a church that ministered to people many churches ignored: drug addicts, prostitutes, the poor, and people of different races and cultures.

When Wilkerson came to our church, I was thirteen. Although I knew I was a Christian, I hadn't been filled with the Holy Spirit, and that bothered me. In fact, I was afraid it might never happen. Brother Wilkerson was known as a "Holy Ghost preacher." In addition to inviting sinners to come forward to accept Jesus into their hearts, he challenged every Christian to be filled with the Holy Spirit. When he gave the invitation every night during the revival at our church, I practically ran to the altar, knelt, and asked God to fill me with the Holy Spirit. I stayed until midnight, praying to be filled with the Holy Spirit. But night after night, I went home disappointed.

The last night of the revival, I decided I was going to stay until the Lord filled me with the Holy Spirit, no matter how long it took. All my life I'd heard my dad and others teach that inviting Jesus into your heart was absolutely necessary for the forgiveness of our sins and the reward of spending eternity with God in heaven, but God offers even more: we can be filled with His Spirit. I desperately wanted that to happen in my life.

On that final night, the altar was lined with people who came forward and were filled with the Holy Spirit, which always caused great rejoicing from those who had knelt beside them. Even as I prayed and struggled, I heard the shouts of joy from those to my left and right. I wanted what they had received, but by midnight I was the last seeker at the altar. Everyone else had left except an elderly man named Brother Brown and a little lady named Sister Angel. These two dear people stayed to pray with me.

After another hour passed, Brother Brown got up to leave. He assured me he would continue praying that God would fill me with His Spirit, but the sound of the big church door closing followed by the rumble of his car felt like a bad omen. I wondered, *Maybe it'll never happen. Maybe for whatever reason God doesn't want to give me this gift.*

All my life I'd been taught that if I repented of my sins and got baptized, I would be filled with the Holy Spirit. I had done both. I'd also been taught that all I need to do is ask God for this gift, and He would give it to me. I'd done a lot of asking, and once again I was on my knees asking for this precious gift. But long after midnight, I was all alone except for Sister Angel, and nothing seemed to be happening. After another hour, she told me she had to leave. She explained that she had kids at home who needed to go to school in a few hours. From the look on her face, it was obvious she felt anguished about leaving me alone, and I felt even worse that she had stayed so long with nothing to show for it.

Then it happened.

As I heard the sound of her footsteps fade as she walked toward the back of the church, I felt the power of God's Spirit flow through me, and I experienced the fullness of the Holy Spirit! As soon as she heard my joy-filled praise, she came running up to the altar. That's when I also learned that God must have a great sense of humor. When Sister Angel got excited, her P's came out accompanied with a small spray of spit. At that moment, she got close to give me a big hug and began shouting "Praise Him! Praise Him!"—and I got a shower. It was a special kind of baptism! I call it "praise in my face." I didn't mind at all because she was so happy for me, and I was relieved to finally receive this wonderful gift from God.

From that moment, my life was changed forever. At school, the kids had given me a hard time about being a Christian, and it bothered me. But when I went to school the next day and heard their sarcastic remarks, I no longer cared what they thought of me. I attribute this change to the power that the Holy Spirit gives us over anything that gets between us and the Lord. Previously, I had been a little embarrassed and self-conscious about my faith, but I now experienced a humble boldness. God had given me a new perspective. While I had always loved God, I often let other things take prominence in my life.

Now, my relationship with God was more important than anything. I was, as they say, "all in," because I now experienced the fullness of the Holy Spirit.

I also discovered that my attitude toward kids that made fun of me had changed. I no longer saw them as my enemies. They were lost and needed Jesus. I began to see that God's great purpose is to point the lost to the Savior. Instead of getting upset when they called me "preacher," I just smiled, knowing that they really didn't mean any harm. They were just being kids, and in a way were giving me a compliment because it showed that I wasn't trying to hide my faith in God.

As I look back on how this event changed me, I wonder if Christians worry too much about what people think of them. I certainly worried about others' opinions before I was filled with the Holy Spirit, and of course, at times I still do. Our experience of God's grace gives us love for people who don't know Jesus, and our experience of His power gives us courage to step into their lives to communicate God's matchless love. In our culture today, Christians want to fit in and avoid offending anyone by talking about their faith. Maybe they've seen Christians browbeat or manipulate people to get them to believe in Jesus. That's not at all what I'm advocating! Evangelism isn't just about the message; it's also about the messenger demonstrating compassion, patience, and kindness as we get to know people and share the most wonderful news the world has ever heard.

I'm not sure why I struggled so much to experience the power of the Holy Spirit. Some receive it the moment they ask, and others, like me, don't. As we often say, "The Spirit moves in mysterious ways." Maybe as a young Christian I needed to learn to wait upon the Lord. Or maybe God was testing me to see if I was really serious about receiving His Spirit. I honestly don't know. What I do know is that God is faithful. He can be trusted to deliver on His promises, and He has promised to pour out His Spirit on anyone who asks for it.

I'm grateful that I settled this matter as a boy. It wasn't long after this happened that I faced another big challenge, one that has led many young Christians to question—even reject—all they have been taught about their faith.

I was about to enter junior high.

I'M SECOND FROM THE RIGHT WITH MY
WYNDOTTE CROSS COUNTRY TEAM

CHAPTER 5

The Flying Parson

*E*xperts tell us that a large percentage of adolescents go through some form of rebellion as they approach their teenage years. For preachers' kids, the number is probably even higher. Most survive, getting through those years with little permanent damage . . . other than contributing to a lot of gray hair in their parents. Perhaps because my dad treated me with respect and explained the reasons behind his decisions, I was never very rebellious.

I didn't have time to rebel because I was too busy.

Central Junior High School (for the seventh, eighth, and ninth grades) in Kansas City, Kansas, was the biggest junior high school in the city and one of the largest in the entire state. The sprawling brick building on 15th Street would be my academic home for the next three years. Virtually all incoming seventh-graders were intimidated, so it's no wonder that a skinny preacher's kid who grew up rather late felt a measure of anxiety. I must not have let my fears show, though, because my classmates elected me president of the seventh-grade class. From the moment I walked into the cavernous building, I hit the ground running. Literally.

As soon as classes started in junior high, I wanted to play football. The problem was that I was too small, so I joined the cross country team. When basketball season rolled around and I realized I was dwarfed by the other boys trying out for the team, I made a strategic decision: I would become the manager for the basketball team. I went to every practice and game, and I stayed late to pick up all the towels and throw them in the laundry and put away all the equipment. On game days I arrived early to set out all the uniforms, and after they were washed I hung them all back up. In the spring, I ran track. My specialty was the hurdles. I wasn't very fast, but I had really good form, wasting little time clearing the barriers so that I was able to hold my own against the boys who were really fast. That's how I got the nickname, "the Flying Parson"—it was a term of respect rather than ridicule.

As a ninth-grader, I was elected president of the student council. I also played trombone in the band, which included the marching band and the pep band that played at all our basketball games. For good measure I joined UNESCO, a club that promotes science and culture. I was also a member of the Big Reel Club. Whenever a teacher wanted to show a movie in class, it was my job to go to the audio-visual room to check out the film projector and take it to the classroom where I threaded the sixteen-millimeter film through all its appropriate loops. All the teacher had to do was turn out the lights and start the movie. When the film started, I ran back to my own class, and when the film was over, I went back to retrieve the projector and return it to the audio-visual room.

On one occasion when my parents attended teacher conferences at school, my teacher cautioned my parents with a note of exasperation in her voice, "Tommy is just way too busy. He's involved in too many programs. I think you might want to get him to cut back a little."

My mom's answer taught me an important lesson I've practiced throughout my ministry. She explained politely but firmly, "We've taught Tommy that you don't grow by subtraction, but by addition. He'll be just fine."

My mom always told it like it is, and I'm not sure my teacher appreciated it. My busyness was no accident. My parents always encouraged me to get involved—to jump with both feet into everything I did. Their goal wasn't to keep me out of trouble. The real reason they encouraged me to stay busy was because they knew we have only one life to live, so why not live it to the fullest? Why sit around waiting for things to happen when you can make them happen?

Being busy was no guarantee that I would avoid teenage rebellion, but it helped. A lot of good things were happening in my life, but around this time, I began to see some cracks in the foundation of my faith—or at least in the lives of some people who seemed to be doing so many great things for the Lord.

I didn't rebel against God, but I was embarrassed by the church, more specifically the excesses that I began to see in the well-known and highly-successful evangelists. In a way, you could say I was rebellious—I rebelled against Christian leaders who cared more about their reputations than the people in their audiences. I think I'm on firm ground with this kind of rebellion because Jesus felt the same way about the Pharisees. I wanted to see my friends find the Lord, but I didn't want to invite them to some of the revivals we held because I believed they would be turned off by the guest preachers. I wasn't sure what to do, but God gave me a solution. The local Youth for Christ organization regularly held city-wide meetings, and I invited my friends to them. I knew they would be presented with the gospel, but without all the stuff that I thought would turn them off to faith.

What do I mean by "the stuff?" I want to be very careful to avoid being disrespectful, because most of the evangelists who came through our town were wonderful men of God, men like William Branham, Gordon Lindsay, and Jack Coe. These were great preachers who set up huge tents, like the ones used at circuses, that held thousands of people, and thousands attended and invited Christ into their hearts. That's nothing to be embarrassed about. These men were legends, and I got to see them up close because they stayed in our home.

They also conducted the most amazing healing services. With my own eyes, I saw people healed from serious illnesses. With extraordinary spiritual perception, the evangelists even described the clothing and the physical condition of people in the audience—people they hadn't seen and didn't know. I witnessed this first-hand, and it was truly miraculous.

It's very easy to put people with such powerful gifts on a pedestal and forget they're really human. These were the best of men, but still, they were men at best. Actually, it wasn't their greatness that inspired me but their weakness. If God could use flawed people like them, maybe, just maybe, He could use me, too.

Not all the traveling evangelists were as noble and godly as these three. I would have loved to have taken my friends to miracle services. In fact, I believed that even the most skeptical sinner would see the miraculous power of God and become convinced that Christianity is true, but some of the evangelists spent too much time asking the crowds for money. I have nothing against raising money for ministry, but some of their appeals went on forever. People came to these services expecting healing, but sometimes the preachers made false claims. What really bothered me was the way some of the evangelists seemed to compete with each other about who had the biggest tent and the biggest crowd.

This was my crisis of faith: I was deeply troubled by the excesses I saw. I'd grown up revering these men, and to be fair, I believe thousands are in the kingdom because of their preaching. But that doesn't make all they were doing right. As my doubts grew, I began to wonder about these things.

Thankfully, I could talk to my dad about anything. As I was struggling with these questions, I went to him and poured my heart out to him about the offerings, the questionable healings, and the obvious pride and competition among some of them. At the end, I told him, "Dad, I don't believe in some of the things I've seen at those big tent meetings."

"Well, Tommy. What *do* you believe?" he wisely countered.

"I believe that Jesus saves."

He smiled, "Then why don't you preach it, and don't worry about other things."

That's what I've done since that day. My dad's willingness to listen rather than argue, and then encourage me to preach the gospel, put everything in perspective. I believe in all the gifts of the Holy Spirit, and I've experienced them in my life and ministry. I'm fully convinced they're offered to us today. With God's help and thousands of faithful, generous people, I've raised a lot of money for the purpose of reaching people for Jesus, getting them filled with the Spirit, and helping them to get back on their feet. With God's help and thousands of faithful, generous people, I've raised a lot of money for the purpose of reaching people for Jesus, getting them filled with the Spirit, and helping them to get back on their feet. I'm grateful for the way the churches I've pastored have grown, and for the influence they have had on the communities around them.

Having gotten these questions out of the way, the Flying Parson was ready to fly again. This time on his own.

FIRST REVIVAL MEETING AT THE AGE OF 16
IN SEMINOLE, TEXAS 1953

CHAPTER 6

Time to Start Preaching

*W*hen I was growing up, we had church Sunday morning and Sunday evening, and on Wednesday night we had a prayer meeting. During one of those services, I felt the need to go forward and pray. As I was praying, I clearly felt that God was speaking to me. I've never heard God speak to me in an audible voice, but I clearly sensed that on this occasion that He was telling me it was time for me to start preaching.

Later that night when I got home, I told my dad what God was telling me to do, and his answer wasn't very encouraging. "Let's just pray about it, Tommy."

I seldom challenged my dad, but on this occasion, I protested, "But Dad, we've been praying about it since I was thirteen! I'm sixteen, and it's time for me to do something about it."

It was true. When I was thirteen, I felt God calling me to be a preacher. Of course, my dad was thrilled and told me to keep praying and listening, and God would let me know when to start. A few weeks later, my dad drove to Texas to visit his mom, who was sick. My dad's brother-in-law, who had been a missionary to India, was also there. When my grandma started to get better, my dad decided it was time to go home. As he was backing out of the driveway and all the family members were waving to him, his brother-in-law yelled, "Why don't you get Tommy to come down and hold a revival for me?"

My dad was puzzled. He asked his brother-in-law how he knew I felt called to preach.

"I didn't," came the reply. "I don't even know why I said that."

My dad took this as confirmation that my call to preach was genuine, and over the next three years, I regularly sought God's guidance about when I should start preaching. When my dad continued to tell me, "Keep praying," I felt frustrated . . . really frustrated. I must have badgered him enough that finally he agreed that it was time for me to begin my career as a preacher. He even took it a step further.

With his help, I was invited to hold a revival in Seminole, Texas—far out on the west Texas prairie. It's oil country with some big farms and ranches. At the time, Seminole was a little town of about 7,000 people, and the church where I preached my first sermon had about seventy who attended regularly. My dad told me, "If you're going to hold a revival, you're going to need an organ." He shopped around and found a Hammond spinet for about $1,500. I got a loan so I could buy it. In addition to the organ, I played the trombone and the accordion—an instrument I'm convinced the devil plays in hell! I was a regular one-man band, and my performance would guarantee a big crowd because people would want to come out and see the boy preacher who played so many instruments. Believe it or not, I could play the piano, the organ, and the accordion all at once. It was quite a sight!

As I got ready to leave for Seminole, Dad told me, "We've got to find a way to get you there with all those instruments."

My dad bought a used Jeep station wagon, first making sure the organ, trombone, and accordion would fit in the back. The night before I was to leave, I packed everything in the Jeep. As I went to bed, I overheard my mom and dad talking quietly at the kitchen table. Apparently, my mom had had a dream the night before, and she was convinced it was a vision of the future.

"It seemed so real," she said with alarm in her voice as she told Dad about her dream. "The Jeep was flipped over on its side. The wheels were still turning and all the musical instruments were shattered over the highway. It was awful, and I'm so worried about Tommy driving all that distance by himself!"

"No, that wasn't a vision," my dad assured her, and then he used his trademark humor to try to calm her down. "You just ate too much pizza last night."

But Mom didn't laugh.

I was so excited that I could barely sleep, but I must have dozed off because the alarm startled me awake. I quickly got dressed and headed downstairs to the kitchen where my mom had cooked a big breakfast of eggs, bacon, and pancakes. She may have believed it would be my last meal, but all I could think about was hopping into the Jeep and driving to Texas. I wanted to get there in time to set everything up before preaching my first sermon. I quickly polished off the last slices of bacon and headed out the door where my dad was waiting for me. He reminded me, "Be careful, son, and just do your best. God will take care of the rest."

My mom followed me out the front door and gave me a big hug. I was off on my incredible adventure, enjoying the feeling of being on my own and following God's call to the ministry. With two days of driving ahead of me, I had plenty of time to practice my sermons and plan the different numbers to play on my instruments. I also prayed that people would accept Jesus as their Savior, because that's the reason I wanted to be a preacher. I had a passion for the lost, and now I had the opportunity to invite people to come forward and receive Jesus as their Savior.

I was only a few miles out of town when I heard a car honking behind me. I wondered if I was going too slow or something was wrong with my Jeep. I looked in the rear view mirror and saw my dad. To keep my mom from having a nervous breakdown from worrying about me, they were driving behind me to make sure I made it safely to Texas! They followed me all the way to Seminole, but wisely, instead of hanging around to hear me preach, they turned around and drove back to Kansas City. My dad knew I needed to do this on my own, and having him looking over my shoulder would make me even more nervous than I already was. And believe me, as the time approached for the first night of the revival, I was scared to death.

That evening, people began to arrive at the church. Before walking in to start playing the organ, I went behind the church and prayed, "God, I don't want to preach the gospel only because my dad is a preacher and my uncles and aunts are preachers. I want to preach because of You. And God, I pray that during this revival, fifty people will find You and twenty-five will be filled with the Holy Spirit. This will be a sign that I'm truly called and anointed to preach the gospel."

Like my dad instructed me, I did my best, and God handled His end of the deal—every night people were saved. After the first week, the pastor asked me to stay and preach another week, but when he asked me to stay for a third week, I almost panicked. I had run out of sermons! I had preached every sermon I had, and now I had to come up with six more! As the third week unfolded, God gave me new sermons, and on the final night, five people accepted Christ and one was filled with the Holy Spirit. That brought the total for the three weeks to exactly fifty new believers and twenty-five filled with the Holy Spirit.

I was thrilled at the way God answered my prayers by giving me new messages, but I also learned something else: I may have limited God by asking for something too small. He said He will give "exceedingly and abundantly above all that I could ask or think" (Ephesians 3:20). God showed me that I could trust Him for everything, so why not dream big dreams? That's what I've done since then.

At this revival, God gave me my life's verse. As a teenager, I was a small kid. I didn't date girls until I was twenty because the only girls my size were in the nursery! I even wadded up socks and stuck them in my shoes so I'd appear taller. When I asked God for fifty people to find the Lord and twenty-five to be filled with the Holy Spirit, I prayed with limited faith. What business does a short, skinny teenager have thinking he could lead a revival? As I was about to walk out of the empty church and get in my Jeep for the long drive home, I noticed a little plaque on the wall. It said: "'Not by might nor by power, but by My Spirit,' says the Lord of hosts" (Zechariah 4:6). From that moment, this became my life verse.

Suddenly, it all made sense to me. It didn't matter if I was three feet tall or seven feet tall or whether I could lift fifty pounds or 500 pounds. I could memorize the entire Bible and craft a thousand beautiful sermons, but none of that makes any difference in the Lord's work. Only by His Spirit will we accomplish what He has called us to do.

As I got in my car to drive home from Seminole, I was on fire! I can't begin to describe the thrill. I had already been invited to speak at another revival—this time in Merkle, Texas, a rugged little town of about 6,000 people—and I couldn't wait to see what God had in store for the people there.

I drove to Merkle with a Jeep full of instruments. Once again, the Holy Spirit moved powerfully as every night people came forward to receive Jesus as their personal Savior. The next stop was Abilene, and God gave us another great revival. The church was packed every night. People were saved and lives were changed. It was truly a remarkable moving of the Holy Spirit. I could hardly believe how, in just a few weeks, I had gone from a scared little kid to a real evangelist God was using to save the lost. I may have only been sixteen years old, but God's Spirit gave me power and clarity beyond my years, and God moved people to turn their lives over to Christ. The first summer of preaching convinced me that this was all I wanted to do with my life. My calling was to serve the Lord by preaching His life-changing gospel.

I've always been amazed at the message of the gospel. It's so simple that a child can understand it, but it's so profound that we'll never fully grasp the depth and wonder of it—at least not on this side of heaven. A new believer can explain that "Jesus died for my sins" and experience the forgiveness and love God wants to shower on every person. I always want my message to be crystal clear, and I want people to be amazed by God's grace. The gospel is the message that the King of Glory stepped out of heaven to die in our place. He received the punishment we deserve so we could receive the acceptance, glory, and honor He deserves. As I developed my messages, I saw that when Paul wrote that "Christ died for our sins according to the Scriptures," he was referring to passages like Isaiah 53 that says of the Messiah: "But he was pierced for our transgressions, he was crushed for our iniquities; the punishment that brought us peace was upon him, and by his wounds we are healed. We all, like sheep, have gone astray, each of us has turned to his own way; and the Lord has laid on him the iniquity of us all" (Isaiah 53:5–6, NIV). When people turn to Christ, they're saying, "Jesus, I can't save myself, and I trust what You've done for me." And when they trust in Him, their hearts are radically transformed and they want to obey and honor the one who gave himself for them. This is the message that changed me from the inside out, and it has gripped my heart every time I preach. We don't earn God's acceptance. It's a free gift of grace. When we experience it, everything changes: our destiny, our identity, our purpose, and our joys.

Soon, the summer was over, and it was time to go back to school.

Tent Meeting, Russell, Oklahoma

MY FIRST TENT MEETING IN
STERLING, TEXAS, 1955

CHAPTER 7

Tempted by Success

*A*s I drove back to Kansas City, I felt a mix of emotions. I was grateful that God had used me, sad that the summer was over, and eager to jump back into my junior year of high school. Soon, I immersed myself in sports, music, clubs, and church—I even found time to do a little homework.

About halfway through my junior year, I began to make plans for the next summer, and as always, I sought my dad's advice on how and where I should schedule revivals. His response surprised me. "Tommy, you need to get a tent." He explained, "Tents give you the freedom to hold a revival practically anywhere you want, and they hold more people than most churches."

I bought a tent that held about 500 people, and I bought 500 canvas folding chairs. This load was far too much for my Jeep to carry, so I traded it for an old mail truck that held the tent, the chairs, my Hammond organ, my trombone, that cursed accordion, and everything else I would need to spend the summer on the road preaching the gospel. I began scheduling revivals for the summer. The first would be held in Sterling, Kansas—population 1,700. Because I had a tent, I didn't need to be sponsored by a local church.

My preparations, though, took a slight detour. Toward the end of the school year, someone told me about a talent contest sponsored by KCTV, Kansas City's CBS affiliate. The winner would receive a free trip to New York City to compete on the nationally televised CBS program, *Arthur Godfrey's Talent Scouts*. Local CBS affiliates all over America conducted their own contests, and the winners would go to New York for the finals.

I decided to enter.

On a hot and muggy Saturday, my dad took me to the television station on East 31st Street. I was ushered into a room with dozens of other nervous candidates ranging in age from a six-year-old girl to a middle-aged women's trio. As I sized up the competition, I didn't think I had a chance to win, but I was never one to back down from a challenge. One by one, we were called into the studio and given three minutes to perform. When they called my name, I breathed a little prayer, walked into the studio, and sang as if my life depended on it. After we all had taken our turns, we were sent home to await the results of the voting by the viewers. Later that night, I got a call from the station: I had won! Sort of . . .

That was only the first round. The top ten vote-getters were invited back the next Saturday to compete again, this time to narrow the field to three finalists. I practiced the rest of the week, hoping against hope that I'd make the top three. After this round, I made the cut again! Now I'd be in the city finals with a chance to go to New York and compete against the best from all over the nation.

That Sunday, my dad announced in church that I had made the finals and encouraged everyone, "Vote for Tommy!"

After a lot of thought and prayer, I chose a new song for the finals, "The Answer Man." The chorus was, "I don't know all the answers, but I know the Answer Man." Whether I won or lost, I would at least use this opportunity to point people to Jesus. At the same time, I've always had a powerful competitive streak in me. I really wanted to win!

Saturday came, and I joined the two other contestants in the green room. We'd gotten to know each other pretty well by then, which kept us from being too nervous. I'd seen both of them perform before, and I knew they were good . . . in fact, really good. For the finals, I decided to accompany myself on my accordion. After a few minutes in the green room, I took it out of its case to practice. I can't say that I wasn't trying to intimidate them a little.

"I didn't know you played the accordion," one of them commented.

"Oh, I just mess around on it a little," I replied. "I hope I don't make any mistakes today."

The director came into the green room and gave us the lineup. The girl who played the violin would be first, followed by a boy who was a tap dancer. I would go last. The director encouraged us to do our best and have fun. We all shook hands and wished each other good luck, and then we waited for the announcer.

The first person's name was called, and she left the room. After a few minutes, we heard the tap dancer's name, and he left to perform. Then I heard, "And now, from Kansas City, please welcome Tommy Barnett!"

I marched into the studio, looked right into the camera, and gave it my best shot. I don't know if it was because I was pretty good or because everyone in my dad's church—by now one of the biggest in the city—voted for me, but the station recorded the largest number of votes ever—and I won! I had won the talent contest, but more importantly, a trip to New York City to appear on television with Arthur Godfrey, a national star! (The only other religious group to make it to his show were The Blackwood Brothers, a gospel quartet unknown at the time but whose exposure on the program turned them into a nationally acclaimed touring group. They later became a backup group for Elvis Presley and would be eight-time Grammy Award winners, in addition to winning 27 Gospel Music Association Dove Awards and five All-American Music Awards.)

When I got the news, I couldn't believe it. I literally jumped for joy as my dad pounded me on the back and told me how proud he was. My mom looked on, smiling through tears of joy. In the midst of our celebration, I looked again at the information about my highly anticipated trip to New York. I was scheduled to be there on the same day I was to start a revival in Sterling, Kansas. I had made the commitment to the revival, so I told my dad I didn't think I should go to New York.

"But son," he pleaded. "You have to go. This could help you reach more people. After you appear on national television, everyone will want to attend your revivals. Billy Graham was vaulted to success by a feature article in the Hearst newspapers. This could push you to the same kind of recognition."

"Let me pray about it," I answered.

I'd learned from my dad that when faced with an important decision, we shouldn't rely on our own wisdom because it might be influenced by what *we* want rather than what *God* wants. I really wanted to go to New York—it was like a dream come true. And Dad was right. Not only would I be a witness for God on the program, but I'd be able to reach more people for the gospel than I would in Sterling, Kansas.

I asked God to show me what He wanted me to do, and it was clear that He wanted me to honor my commitment to hold the revival in Sterling. It was if He were saying to me, "Put Me first—I want you to hold the tent meeting."

BILLBOARD

When I explained to my dad what God had told me, he wasn't pleased. I completely understood. He wanted to see me succeed as an evangelist, and I knew him well enough that it wasn't about fame. He believed the national exposure would give me greater opportunities to reach the lost.

When I told my friends that I wasn't going to New York, they thought I was crazy. As soon as school got out, I loaded my mail truck and drove three hours to Sterling. When I pulled into town and found the vacant lot I'd arranged to use for the revival, I found two guys and paid them to help me set up my tent, move the organ to the front of the tent, and line all 500 chairs into neat rows stretching from one side to the other. I'd sent notices ahead to be placed in local business-es and in church bulletins, so now all I had to do was wait until the tent filled up so I could do what I loved best: tell people about Jesus and invite them to come forward and turn their lives over to Him. I had sacrificed an opportunity to perform on television to be there, and I was sure it would be a success.

In a town of 1,700 people, forty showed up.

As the time to start approached and I looked at the almost empty tent, I was devastated, but I knew this was where God wanted me to be. At the beginning of the service, I stood up in front of the little group of people scattered throughout my big tent, strapped on my accordion, and began singing "The Answer Man." I couldn't help but think about where I could have been that very moment—walking into a seventy-story CBS building on East 52nd Street in New York, into an elevator and up to the sixtieth floor to the famous Studio 21 where I would have appeared on the number one television program in the nation. Over the years I've learned that when you take a stand for what's right, you don't always get the reward you think you deserve, at least not right away. Maybe that's because the Lord wants to test us. This is especially true for leaders who often have to make tough, unpopular decisions.

I preached my sermon to those forty people, and a couple came forward to accept Christ. I returned the next night, and the tent was half full. We had a wonderful service. People found the Lord and were filled with the Holy Spirit. In fact, from that point on, the tent was packed almost every night. I stayed for two weeks. I have no idea where all the people came from (probably from neighboring towns as their friends told them about the revival), but they came. I realized that my job is to obey and remain faithful, and God will take care of the rest. Even if only a handful of people showed up every night, it still would have been the right thing to continue with the revival because that's exactly where God wanted me.

After two weeks, some men helped me pack the tent and all the other equipment into my old mail truck, and I drove to Duncan, Oklahoma, a small city of just under 20,000. This revival was sponsored by a successful Assembly of God church pastored by Haskell Rogers, and once again, the Holy Spirit moved powerfully. Over two weeks, hundreds of people accepted Jesus and were filled with the Holy Spirit. Something else moved, and I'll never forget it.

About halfway through the revival, a thunderstorm woke me up in the middle of the night. Oklahoma is notorious for its fierce storms. The area is often referred to as "Tornado Alley," and as it approached, I could tell this storm packed a powerful punch. As the wind rattled the window panes in the parsonage where I was staying, my first thought was the tent. I woke up the pastor. He called a few of the men from the church, and we raced to the tent, grabbing the ropes to keep it from blowing away. Miraculously, God spared the tent, although it was ripped in a few places. A few of the ladies showed up the next day and sewed it up, and we were back in business that night.

The revival in Duncan was so successful that they asked me to stay for a third week, but I'd already committed to holding a revival in Dallas. Jack Coe, one of the first of the renowned faith healers, had started a church there—the Dallas Revival Center—and he asked me to hold a revival. After we wrapped things up in Duncan on a Saturday night, I drove about three hours to Dallas, arriving well after midnight, to preach on Sunday. Brother Coe emphasized healing, and I stayed true to my calling to invite people to accept Jesus as their Savior and to be filled with the Holy Spirit. We had a wonderful series of meetings in the tent that we set up next to the church.

That's how I spent the rest of the summer. Setting up my tent, playing all my musical instruments, preaching the gospel, and then packing everything up in the old mail truck and driving to the next town. I loved every minute of it. It may seem unusual today for a seventeen-year-old kid to be so serious about preaching, but at the time, young evangelists were quite the thing. Another teenage evangelist was called "Little David," and some older readers might remember the curly-haired kid preacher, Marjoe Gortner. They preached to thousands, while I preached to anywhere from dozens to a few hundred, but I didn't care. I was never concerned about numbers. I just loved the adventure of taking the gospel to people who needed it.

MY PICTURE TAKEN FOR A RECORD ALBUM COVER

DUNCAN, OKLAHOMA, TENT MEETING

CHAPTER 8

Sandstorm

I thoroughly enjoyed the summer of revivals. I drove the mail truck loaded with the tent and all my musical instruments to town after town. I couldn't have been happier! Sometimes I finished a revival, hopped in the truck and drove all night to get to another one that was starting the next day. I often had to change into my "preaching suit" in the restroom of gas stations.

One of my favorite places to preach was my uncle's church in Seminole, Texas. Like my dad, my uncle was passionate about getting people saved. He'd spent about fifteen years as a missionary to India, and he captivated me with tales of killing poisonous snakes and man-eating leopards that ravaged the villages. He also introduced me to one of my favorite dishes: Indian curry and rice. I couldn't get enough of it.

I parked the truck in the driveway of his parsonage just minutes before a monumental sandstorm arrived. I'd never seen anything like it—the massive cloud of sand and dirt blotted out the sun. We barricaded ourselves inside the parsonage all day, but the windblown sand got in through every tiny crack and opening. Sand was everywhere—in our hair, in our food, in the church, even inside our clothes. The storm subsided just in time for the first night of the revival, but only a few people showed up. The low attendance was completely understandable because people were busy cleaning their houses! That didn't discourage me because I knew if I was faithful, God would handle the rest. And He did. The next night the high school football star walked into the church just as we were starting the music. After I preached, I gave the altar call, and the burly football player stepped out of his seat, almost raced to the altar, and prayed to accept Jesus as his Savior. In Texas, few people wield as much influence as the high school football star . . . except the homecoming queen, and she showed up the following night and turned her life over to the Lord. For the rest of the week, the church was packed.

One night a little thirteen-year-old girl was filled with the Holy Spirit and immediately began speaking in a heavenly language. Quietly and softly, she prayed in earnest for several minutes. After she was finished praying, one of my uncle's sons—a boy of about nine or ten years old—tugged on my uncle's coattails and whispered, "Daddy, she was speaking in Hindi!"

The little girl had never been to India and had no idea she was speaking in one of the major dialects where my uncle had served as a missionary. We were all amazed at this miraculous "coincidence." An even bigger miracle occurred after she finished praying. She stood up and announced, "I believe God is calling me to be a missionary to India." My uncle was thrilled that this little girl would eventually continue the work he had begun, and I was grateful that God used a teenage evangelist like me to add yet another worker to His Kingdom.

I spent the rest of the summer doing what I loved doing and still love: preaching the gospel. I'm thrilled every time I see someone find the Lord. This was my second summer of preaching. I had developed enough sermons to keep me going if the revival lasted more than a couple of weeks, but really, I only had one sermon: "God loves you, and He sent His Son to take the punishment for your sins. You can come forward and receive Him into your heart and be saved." We might come up with a lot of different ways to say it, but essentially, that's our only message to the world. Jesus saves!

It was, by all measures, a wonderful summer. You might think some success would go to my head, especially as young as I was. But I had an advantage that kept me from the temptation of pride.

DAD AND ME

CHAPTER 9

Learning from the Best

I'm not a self-made man. In fact, I don't even like the term because it sounds arrogant. I'm a product of the great preachers I've been blessed to know over the years. For example, the late evangelist Oral Roberts came to visit me in Phoenix and taught me to have faith—seed faith, which means that God can take something small and make great things with it. When people see Tommy Barnett, they see a little bit of Oral Roberts.

They also see a little bit of Dr. David Yonggi Cho, founder of South Korea's Yoido Full Gospel Church, the world's largest congregation with more than 700,000 members. I've served on Dr. Cho's board for more than thirty years. He taught me how to believe God to build big churches. A big church can influence the city—when a big church speaks, the city listens. Big churches aren't just about numbers; they're about influence. Because of the influence of Dr. Cho, I've always wanted to pastor a church that had an impact on the entire city.

When people see me, they see a little bit of Dr. Jack Hyles, the Independent Baptist preacher from Hammond, Indiana. That may surprise a lot of people because he and I didn't have a lot in common, especially when it comes to the gifts of the Holy Spirit. Although I never met him, I had the opportunity to hear him speak one time, and I'm pretty sure I listened to every message he ever gave (and I listened to them on cassettes, if you remember those). Dr. Hyles taught me principles of integrity, honor, and faithfulness—the qualities that really matter.

But the person you see most clearly when you see me is my father, Hershel Barnett. People sometimes ask me how I learned to preach. That's easy. I learned from my dad. He was a great preacher, but even more, he was a great man—I like to think a little of his heart and his skill rubbed off on me. He encouraged me to preach, often taking me to one of the missions in downtown Kansas City so I could preach to the homeless men who showed up for services. It was my favorite place to preach because men responded every night when I gave the altar call, and that encouraged me. In fact, one of the most important things I learned from my dad was how to give an altar call.

My dad taught me the importance of honesty—to always tell the truth no matter what—and he taught it by example. My dad wasn't exactly politically correct because it never seemed to bother him when people made fun of him for being a "hellfire and brimstone" preacher. He stood against a number of sins that devastated people but were widely accepted, even among Christians, especially alcohol. He was a principled man and believed he was addressing the evil of liquor as a way to preach the gospel and introduce people to Jesus.

At one point when my father was a young preacher, it was rumored that President Roosevelt hosted drinking parties in the White House, and Dad preached against this practice. Some leaders in the Assemblies of God hierarchy called Dad into their offices to ask him to tone down his attacks on the president. He stared at the men who held power in our denomination. He reached into his wallet, took out his ministerial credentials that officially licensed him to preach, politely put them on the table, and then turned and walked to the door. Fortunately, one of the presbyters went after him and gently grabbed him by the shoulder. "Wait, preacher," he said. "You don't have to do that. We want you to stay and keep preaching."

When I saw my dad take stands like this, it strengthened my conviction to be bold. There's a temptation to tell people what they want to hear, but my dad could never do that . . . and neither can I. A few years ago, a guest preacher made a sarcastic reference to "Adam and Steve" as he was making a point about homosexuality. Later that week I got a letter from a woman in our church who explained that her son was a homosexual. She wrote that she prayed for his salvation every day, but when the preacher tried to make a joke out of homosexuality, it broke her heart. I knew she was right. I believe this lifestyle goes against God's design, but I've always treated people with respect, whether I agree with their lifestyle or not. God sent us to heal, not to hurt. My dad never pulled any punches when he preached about sin. He told the truth, but he also loved every person who walked through the doors of his church.

My dad also taught me about compassion. A lot of church leaders believe Dad was the father of the bus ministry—at one time running more than ten buses to pick up children all over the city. He loved people who are hurting—the people nobody else wanted in their churches. Some people criticized him for filling our Sunday school with kids who came from rough homes and didn't know how to behave in church. I'll never forget what he told me after someone chewed him out for spending so much time and energy on the bus ministry: "Those little kids grow up. God saves them, and soon their parents start coming to church, and God saves them, too. That's how you build a church, Tommy. Jesus said He didn't come for the righ-teous but for the sinners."

I got my passion for lost people from my dad. He taught me how to give an altar call. My dad never held a service without inviting people to come to the altar to accept Christ. Sometimes the invita-tion went on a little long, and not just because "Just as I Am" has so many verses. He wanted to give even the most reluctant person the opportunity to find the Lord. As far as I'm concerned, that's the most important thing a church can do. If we don't do that, we're just anoth-er club trying to do nice things for the community. I believe that the nicest thing we can do as a church is to get as many as possible into the Kingdom. I watched my dad lead people to Christ from the time I was a little boy until I was on my own as a young evangelist.

Serving the Lord as an evangelist or pastor is a wonderful privi-lege, but it's also hard work. My dad taught me that in order to live up to that calling, you had to be disciplined. I saw him work long hours, visit countless homes, and then go to the hospital to call on people who were sick. But it wasn't just by watching him that I learned dis-cipline. It may not be as fashionable today, but when I was a boy he "administered" discipline whenever I needed it, which was often. For example, no matter what, I was required to practice the piano for an hour every day. An hour—every day! From the moment I got home from school, I wasn't allowed to do anything else until I finished my hour at the piano. Of course, I hated playing the piano and often sneaked off to play baseball with my buddies. For several years when I was a boy, I got more than a few spankings because I refused to prac-tice. But my dad had such a tender heart that after he sent me up to my room, he came to talk with me. "Son, I love you," he always began. "I don't want to discipline you, and sometimes maybe I spank you too hard. Please forgive me." Then he reached into his pocket, took out a couple of quarters and handed them to me. "Now, why don't you go get yourself an ice cream cone."

I started crying, we'd hug, and I'd tell him how sorry I was for disobeying him. I never resented the spankings because I knew I was wrong, and he was following through on what he said he would do if I didn't practice the piano. I somehow knew that he disciplined me because he wanted me to make something of myself. He saw the potential in me even when I didn't, and he cared enough about me to turn me into a decent piano player. His strategy worked. I learned how to play the piano, the organ, and that blasted accordion, and I was able to use those skills for the Lord. Instead of having to hire a pianist or organist when I began my calling as an evangelist, I unloaded my Hammond spinet from the truck. To this day I'm convinced a lot of people came out to see the young "one-man band!"

Thanks, Dad!

Finally, my dad taught me to love the church and how to build a great church. After he held a revival in Kansas City where the Spirit moved in a mighty way, the sponsoring church asked him to become their pastor. It was a little church with barely a hundred people showing up on Sunday morning. I watched him over the years—forty in all—build a church that survived a flood and two fires. By the time he died, the church had grown to more than 1,700 people, the largest in the city. He was so popular in the community that he was elected to the school board and served for sixteen years. He even ran for mayor and almost got elected, but some speculate that his position on the sale of alcohol cost him a lot of votes. The state legislature eventually passed a law making it legal to sell alcohol, but that didn't stop my dad. He found a clause in the state constitution that overturned this law, making him very unpopular to all the drinkers. The *Kansas City Star* ran a cartoon of him leaning over "Barnett's Bar" with a shotgun aimed at a guy standing at the bar with a glass in his hand. The caption read, "You'll drink sarsaparilla and like it!"

NEWSPAPER CARTOON DURING MY DAD'S BATTLE WITH THE KANSAS LIQUOR VOTE

My dad was a wonderful man who poured himself into the lives of others, but he always had time for me. He came to every track meet and cheered me on no matter where I finished. He attended all my school activities and made sure I knew he loved me. My mom was a great Bible teacher in her own right and always told me, "Tommy, you can be anything you want to be, and you'll be the best."

When you look at me, I trust you'll see the evidence of wonderful parents and godly preachers who had a powerful impact on me, and I'm grateful for that rich heritage. When I graduated from high school, it was time for the next stop—Bible college.

DEDICATION OF THE PHOENIX CHILDREN'S
BUILDING IN HONOR OF MY DAD

He Sings, Tells the Gospel

Evangelist, 22, Seeks to Fill 'Youth's Vacuum'

BOB DART

Barnett is young in evangelist. He's only 22, a preacher with athletics and an appeal. His second area visit, series of tent meetings on adway at Bulkhead, is now way.

my says his father, Herwas a "hell-fire, brimpreacher" who didn't be in sparing the rod. "It dad to whip me," Tommy ies, "but I earned his rect. It was discipline balced with love."

In the late 30s, Herschel was crusader for his own church Kansas City. But his son preferred baseball to piano practice—dawn to dusk he would play ball on a lot next to the church, until dad appeared to march him home.

Tommy Barnett was born in Electra, Tex., but his family moved to Kansas when he was 4. It was there Tommy "felt the call of my life. Dad's work impressed me. I accompanied him on visits to the sick and the dying."

SO, AT 16, he became the youngest licensed evangelist of his church in the Kansas district.

Until high school graduation, he spent summers preaching. Then came a year at South-ern Bible Institute in

went into the record business. At a western recording studio, accompanied by bass, celeste, guitar, organ and piano, the young evangelist made long-play albums under his own label, Barnett. On tour, Tommy sells these records at the close of each meeting.

His idol is miler Wes Santee. A hurdle man in school track, Tom was once called "The Flying Parson." He builds his youth sermons around athletics, with titles like "Champions" and "Hurdling to Hell!"

Tommy has preached in the Bahamas, Mexico, Canada and most of the United States. In Hollywood, he met actress Jane Russell and briefly turned actor for a short television commercial, filmed by Jane's brother, Jamie. He uses this film on tour in TV commercials.

Evangelist Tommy's greatest adventure is coming this fall. In just three months, he begins a journey around the world.

TRAVELING companion will be a movie camera. He'll combine preaching with photography, the trip to be financed through sales of his recordings. He plans tours of America following the global hop.

Today, his athletics are limited to golf and swimming. Beams Tommy, "I shot a par game recently."

He values his Red Cross certificate received in life saving.

But he believes many lives are saved through youth evangelism. hellfire message is con-

CHAPTER 10

Off to School, Out of School

*D*uring the years I was in high school, a lot of young men and women didn't go on to college, often because they didn't have the money, but also because a college degree wasn't necessary for them to pursue their career choice. In the 1950s people could graduate from high school and get a good job. In fact, it wasn't unusual for a young man to graduate, start working in a factory or some other business, get married, raise a family, and stay in that same job until he retired. Unless you had wealthy parents or were a veteran and could go to college free on the GI Bill, you hardly gave college a thought. In fact, from my high school graduating class, only about eight percent of the men and five percent of the women earned college degrees.

In my denomination, a college degree wasn't required for people who wanted to become pastors, but some type of formal education beyond high school was strongly encouraged. As I've described, during my senior year, I began lining up revival meetings for the summer after I graduated, and I considered scheduling them into the fall. I had enjoyed some success as an evangelist and felt this was my calling, and I was making a decent living. As much as my parents supported my call to preach, they also knew I would benefit from additional education. One night they presented me with a strong case for going to college. They even had one already picked out for me: Southwestern Bible College (now Southwestern Assemblies of God University) in Waxahachie, Texas—it was the school they had attended.

Even though all I wanted to do was preach, their wise counsel made sense to me. In those days, Bible colleges offered two-year degree programs, and after students finished, they could either become officially licensed to pastor a church or transfer to a four-year college degree and perhaps go to seminary. I was convinced that two years of studying the Bible would help me become a better preacher, and besides, I loved my parents and knew they only wanted the best for me. I applied to Southwestern and was accepted. I made plans to go there after a summer of revivals.

When the summer ended, I found myself on the seventy-acre campus of Southwestern Bible College with little more than a suitcase and my Bible. Thanks to the success of my two summers of preaching, I'd saved up enough money to cover most of my tuition, room and board, and to buy a new car. From the moment I arrived at the school, I loved being there—or maybe I just loved going to school where everyone was a Christian. We went to chapel every day and heard terrific preaching—sometimes from visiting evangelists and pastors, and sometimes from members of the faculty—and the more I heard, the more inspired I became. I couldn't wait to finish my degree and return to preaching full-time.

Still, my passion for preaching persisted, and while I was a student, I got my chance. During one of my summers as an evangelist, I had preached at a revival for the world-famous evangelist, Jack Coe. His church was just a few miles from the college, and sadly, he passed away shortly after I got to school. His wife was doing her best to keep their church going. She asked me to preach at a weekend of services as part of the outreach of Southwestern, and I jumped at the opportunity. During those services, God moved in a special way, and we saw hundreds of people get saved.

A few days after those services, I got a call from Mrs. Coe. She asked if I would serve alongside her and preach there on weekends. *Would* I? She couldn't have offered me a better gift. For the rest of my first year in college, I preached every weekend, and we shared a wonderful ministry together. Students from Southwestern often attended, and many of them were involved in outreach activities that brought the unsaved to hear the gospel. Over the course of the year, hundreds of people accepted Jesus as their Savior. By the end of the school year, I made a big decision. I wouldn't be returning to college. I loved the school, but I had already learned a lot from others like my dad and the preachers who came to our home. I had seen what God had done through my preaching, and I wanted to get back to what God had called me to do.

Because I never finished college, I pushed myself to learn from every situation and every person. Whether you're trying to buy a tent to hold revival meetings or buying a hospital from a group of Catholic nuns, you can learn a lot if you pay attention. Graduating from college with a degree is just the beginning. Maybe that's why they call the graduation ceremony "commencement"—because your *real* education is about to commence. Whether you have a college degree or barely made it through high school—whether you're in your twenties or like me, a little older than twenty!—never stop learning. I love the verse in Romans where Paul talks about the "renewing of the mind" in order to discern God's will. I take that to mean we should always keep studying, applying what we learn to real life, and most importantly, remaining open to what God wants to teach us.

I soon learned that God still had a lot to teach me . . . and a gift to give me.

MARJA IN HER MODELING YEARS

CHAPTER 11

Marja

I'll never forget the revival at Elmira, New York. Most revivals are planned for one week, but this one was scheduled for two weeks. The church was packed every night with hundreds finding the Lord and being filled with the Holy Spirit. After it was over and I prepared to leave, the pastor asked me to stay one more week. For the following week, I had scheduled a revival in Cumberland, Maryland. I prayed and called the pastor of the church in Cumberland to ask if we could postpone the meetings, and he generously agreed to wait.

Once again, the Spirit moved miraculously in Elmira—the church was so crowded that it's a good thing the fire inspector didn't show up—or maybe he did and got saved! The third week of revival was phenomenal, and the pastor again asked me to stay and preach for another week. Three weeks of preaching every night left me quite hoarse, and I was physically exhausted. Besides, the revival in Cumberland was waiting for me. I told him I just couldn't go on, but that night, I couldn't sleep. I tossed and turned all night. The next morning, the pastor knocked on my door. When I opened it, he told me bluntly, "I think you missed God."

With no hesitation I answered, "I think I did, too." We announced on the radio we were continuing the revival.

That day, I rested up as best as I could and preached to overflow crowds that night. And the next. And the next. God gave me supernatural strength. At the end of the week, the pastor and I knew the Lord wasn't finished—the revival lasted a total of nine weeks! Every week, I called the pastor in Cumberland, and he graciously kept encouraging us to continue. Finally, near the end of the ninth week, he pleaded with me to shut things down in Elmira. I closed the revival on Sunday night, drove all night to Cumberland, rested during the day, and began preaching another revival. This one stretched on every night for five weeks.

During this time I also began preaching at youth camps. All across America, churches and other ministries such as Youth for Christ developed beautiful campgrounds where young people could enjoy the outdoors, meet kids from all over the region, and be challenged to live for Christ. One of the camps was outside Harrisburg, Pennsylvania. Maranatha Camp was the largest youth camp in America, and they invited me to preach. More than 1,500 teenagers attended every night for a week. The special music for the week was provided by a young pianist by the name of Dino Kartsonakis, who would later record fifty albums and host his own television show. He showed up in a billowy, sequined shirt, white slacks, and blue suede shoes. To no one's surprise, he became known as "the Christian Liberace."

To be honest, I also paid a fair amount of attention to how I looked, with my Elvis-style hair (back when I had some) and fancy suits and ties. These church-sponsored camps offered opportunities for spiritual growth, and they gave kids a chance to have some fun.

Revivals and youth camps were popular in that era because every Christian's life was built around the church, and these events broadened people's experiences. Television and the internet have changed all that because now you can flip on the channel or browse online and see the best preaching and teaching, fantastic music, and dramatic productions—all from the comfort of your living room or wherever you have a laptop or smartphone. Why go to a revival when you can listen and watch a gifted preacher delivering a carefully-scripted message supported by world-class musicians and mesmerizing videos? Please don't misunderstand: I'm not being critical. I'll support just about anything in good taste that gets people saved or helps them grow in their faith. However, I think we've lost something because face-to-face contact is essential in the family of God. The writer to the Hebrews commands us: "And let us not neglect our meeting together, as some people do, but encourage one another, especially now that the day of his return is drawing near" (Hebrews 10:25, NLT). Times change, and I'm glad they do. Over the years I've adapted the way I preach and do ministry, but there's no substitute for bringing people together to worship, pray, and sing.

Most of the time, I provided the special music for my revivals, and along the way I was offered a recording contract from Sacred Records. At the time, the record company offered a "Sacred Album of the Month" to a very large list of subscribers, and my album made it to that coveted spot. I also like to tell people that for a while, it was the number one album in the nation, which is true, but needs a little explaining.

A missionary friend invited me to the Philippines to hold a revival, and I agreed to go. It was a terrific series of meetings, and one of the top deejays in that country—a beautiful young woman—came and got saved. I think she also liked me because she began playing my album on her radio program. Pretty soon, it was being played on radio stations all over the Philippines, and it briefly made it to the number one spot. It wasn't exactly Dick Clark's *American Bandstand*, but for a young evangelist, it felt pretty good.

When I got back in the states, I headed west in a new gold and white Dodge convertible, barreling down Route 66 with the top down, my shirt off, radio blaring, and tires humming. I may have been an evangelist who was serious about getting people saved, but I was still a kid, and the temptation of those long, open roads was too much to ignore. More than once the speedometer hit 100 miles per hour. I must have had a guardian angel because one day, just after crossing into California, one of the tires blew out, and the car began sliding into a ditch. My big, shiny convertible tipped precariously and was about to roll over when I cried out, "Oh God, take the wheel!" Miraculously, the car righted itself and landed on all four wheels. It scared me to death! After sitting still for a while to settle my nerves and let my adrenaline level return to something close to normal, I changed tires and drove off—this time a lot more slowly. To commemorate this event, I wrote a song called "He'll Take Over the Wheel." It must have been a pretty good song because a few years ago Carrie Underwood recorded her first single, "Jesus Take the Wheel," and it shot to the top of Billboard's country list, stayed there for six consecutive weeks, and won a Grammy for her. Sad to say, it wasn't the song I wrote.

I held revivals at some of the largest churches in California, including ones in Santa Monica, Pomona, North Hollywood, and San Diego. Every night, we saw huge crowds with hundreds accepting Christ and being filled with the Holy Spirit. I was still young, but God was using me in ways I never could have imagined. And then, just as I was about to go to yet another revival, I got a call from my aunt. My uncle, a pastor in Palo Alto, was crossing the railroad tracks when a train hit his car, killing him instantly. My aunt asked me if I would come and help her keep the church going. I wasn't a pastor, just a young evangelist, but I agreed to at least go and hold a revival for her.

One night in August of 1964, as I was preaching at my uncle's church, I looked toward the back and saw the most beautiful girl

I'd ever seen. She was tall, blonde, and gorgeous. I later learned that she had just arrived from Sweden, and she had been a contestant in the Miss Sweden beauty pageant. She decided to come to America to train to become a flight attendant for Scandinavian Airlines. She supported herself as a nanny for a local family, but there was another reason she came to America. She had grown up under difficult circumstances. She began praying every night at her Lutheran church in Sweden. She felt a hunger she couldn't explain and sought answers at her church. As she prayed, she kept sensing that God was telling her: "If you go to America, you will find Me."

From the moment she walked into the church and took her seat, I preached to one person. When I gave the invitation, she walked down the aisle and knelt at the altar. In those days when someone responded to the altar call, one of the members of the church or a deacon knelt and prayed with the person. On that night I felt called to kneel next to the young woman, ostensibly for all the right spiritual reasons, but maybe her beauty had something to do with it, too.

My dad had always counseled me to avoid dating anyone from my revivals. He warned me that it would damage my reputation. I followed his wise counsel about revivals, but this was different: I was asked to fill the pulpit and help my aunt with the pastoral duties on an interim basis. I couldn't resist going out with this beautiful new believer. My aunt didn't mind because it kept me there helping her. I was twenty-seven years old, and I wanted to get married and have kids. I was beginning to wonder if it would ever happen. And then this lovely young woman, a new Christian, and so fun to be with, walked not only into that church, but also into my life. Her name was Marja.

After three months, I told her, "Honey, forget Scandinavian Airlines. Come fly with me!" And she did. She didn't know what she was getting into, but she would soon find out.

OUR WEDDING DAY

CHAPTER 12

"We Do!"

*D*uring our brief, four-month courtship, I tried to help Marja understand some of the traditions of the church and what it meant to be married to a preacher. For one thing, in that era women in the church—and especially wives of the ministers and evangelists—didn't wear makeup . . . or jewelry . . . or fancy clothes. They were expected to be models of modesty, but Marja had been a model, posing for photographs wearing clothes by designers like Christian Dior and Pierre Cardin. She couldn't understand why she had to wipe off her makeup before going to church and change from a nice tailored dress into a frumpy one that made her look like, well, a preacher's wife.

Marja needed help to understand what her new role would mean, so I decided to enlist my mom. Marja went to Kansas City to stay with my mom and dad while I continued my ministry. I hoped the time with them would give her more insight into what it would be like to be the wife of an evangelist. Everything was new and different to Marja. My mom was very patient with this new Christian who would soon become her daughter-in-law, and Marja has mentioned many times how much it meant to her to experience my mom's kindness and counsel.

Once, Marja was so stressed over all the new requirements that she craved a cigarette. A smoker since her teens—which was common in Sweden—she quit after she got saved, but on this particular day, she really needed a smoke. She quickly realized she had a problem: how do you smoke a cigarette in the parsonage of one of Kansas City's biggest and most highly visible churches? She slipped out the back door to walk to a convenience store where she bought a pack of cigarettes. Back in the parsonage, she locked herself in the bathroom and lit up. My mom could smell the tobacco smoke—it was certainly the first time the distinct aroma had wafted through the parsonage. She started pounding on the bathroom door, pleading with Marja to come out, but Marja was embarrassed . . . and more than a little fearful that she had blown it with her future mother-in-law. Finally, my mom promised that if Marja would come out of the bathroom, she wouldn't tell me about the incident. Marja unlocked the door and walked into the arms of my mom.

My dear mom treated Marja like a queen. Every morning she took a tray of orange juice, coffee, and toast to Marja's room, then handed her a couple of vitamins, adding, "Honey, you're going to need these if you're going to marry Tommy." From her own experience, she knew what it was like to be married to someone intensely dedicated to serving the Lord, and she also knew that Marja would struggle with the public's expectations of being my wife.

There were some funny moments, too. Marja wanted to help with household chores, and she offered to clean the bathroom. My mom had bought a nice brush for scrubbing her back while taking a bath, but Marja used it to scrub the toilet. At that moment, my mom walked past the open bathroom door. She instantly blurted out, "Why are you using my bath brush to clean the toilet?"

Marja was so embarrassed that she burst into tears and slumped to the floor. Instead of trying to correct her, Mom rushed into the bathroom, sat beside her, and put her arm around her. In a few seconds, Mom began laughing. Soon Marja was laughing, too. That's just the kind of person my mom was.

Marja and I planned to get married sometime in the spring. That would give her more time to stay at my parent's home and learn more about being a preacher's wife. As the second week in December rolled around, I was looking forward to my next big trip, this time to the Philippines and India. I was scheduled to leave in only two weeks. As I talked to my dad one day, he surprised me: "Son, you need to take Marja with you."

He could see the stunned look on my face, so he smiled and quickly said, "But you need to marry her first!"

I tried to explain that we didn't have time for a wedding before I left, but he told me, "She'll be fine. Just marry her and take her with you!"

The thought hadn't occurred to me, but when I told Marja, she was all for it. This was going to be the shortest wedding preparation of all time, and there were a couple of disappointments: she realized there wasn't time for the wedding she had dreamed about, and her parents weren't able to come over from Sweden. Still, she was ready to make it work. The first (and probably most important) step was finding the right dress. She had to borrow one from a lady in Dad's church—it was simple, not exactly one you'd see on the cover of a fashion magazine, but it would have to do. I called some of my friends and she called hers to stand up with us at the wedding. In only a few days, we were ready.

On the morning of December 11, 1964, I eagerly anticipated everyone arriving at my dad's church that afternoon. A couple of hours before the ceremony, I called Marja and asked, "Honey, would you go a little light on the makeup?" Today, as I think about my request, I wonder why Marja didn't run out the door. I wanted her to fit the model of a preacher's wife, but I should have been more sensitive . . . especially at that tender moment.

The church was packed with people as I stood at the front and watched as Marja began walking down the aisle. I wondered, *What in the world have I done to this girl? She's from a different culture. She's only been in America a short while, and she knows very little of what she's in for as my wife. How are we going to make this work?*

Years later as we talked about our wedding day, Marja told me that as she walked toward me, she wondered, *What in the world have I gotten into? I never expected to come to America and marry a preacher.*

When we went through our vows, I had a slip of the tongue. I said, "For better or worse, for *preacher* or poorer." A moment later, I was so touched that I started to weep.

Marja whispered, "What's wrong? Why are you crying?"

I smiled, "I'm so happy. These are tears of joy."

After the wedding, everyone was thrilled. All the guests and our friends moved toward the reception, but before Marja and I got there, her friends "kidnapped" her and my friends "kidnapped" me. It was a normal, customary prank young people played on their just-married friends, but of course, it was new—and startling—to Marja. After a long evening of being separated, our friends finally dropped us off about midnight at the Hilton in downtown Kansas City.

The next morning, we got up and went to dad's church for the celebration of the Singing Christmas Tree, with a forty-foot tree and 300 voices. It was quite a beginning to our marriage.

The very next day, Marja and I got on a plane and left the country.

ON SAFARI IN SOUTHERN INDIA, 1964

CHAPTER 13

Honeymoon Safari

*B*efore the ink was dry on our marriage license, I returned to full-time evangelistic work. There wasn't time for a long, relaxed honeymoon because I'd scheduled revivals just after the wedding. The first trip was to the Philippines where missionaries had set up revivals, but this time, I wasn't on my own. I had a companion—Marja, my wife of twenty-four hours. On the way, we squeezed in a three-day honeymoon in Hawaii. Marja was excited about stopping in Hawaii, but not so much about hanging out with missionaries.

After a wonderful but brief time in Hawaii, we got on a plane. When it touched down in Manila, the temperature and humidity were both in the nineties. We transferred to another flight that took us to Iloilo City, one of the largest cities in the Philippines, and a few degrees even hotter and more humid. The missionary couple met us, and we packed our luggage and all of us into their van (with no air conditioning) for the ten-mile trip to their home. The journey took us almost an hour due to the heavy traffic and narrow streets. Before leaving Hawaii, Marja had treated herself to a permanent, but by the time we arrived at the missionaries' home, her beautiful blonde hair hung like wet straw on her shoulders—and her demeanor matched the listlessness of her hair!

After a sparse meal, they showed us to our tiny upstairs room that would be our love nest during the revival. Finally, after more than twenty hours of travel, we had some privacy . . . except that the next morning at six o'clock—and every morning—they banged the dinner bell to call us for breakfast. Welcome to the ministry, Marja!

The story gets better, or worse, depending on your perspective. After the revival in Iloilo City, we flew to India where I was to preach in one of the largest soccer stadiums in Bangalore, India's third largest city. But there was a big problem: just before we arrived, a major typhoon struck and destroyed the soccer stadium, along with the homes of many people who might have attended the revival, so it had to be canceled.

PREACHING AT AN INDIAN VILLAGE

The missionary who had organized the revival wanted to make up for the disappointment, so he arranged for Marja and me to take a hunting safari. A Muslim cook and guide drove us to a hunting compound far off into the desolate jungles of southern India. As a kid who spent many summers on the Texas plains catching snakes and hunting all sorts of animals, I was thrilled. In my childhood I'd heard heart-pounding stories of hunters tracking Bengal tigers, and now I would have a chance to do it myself. Marja, to no one's surprise, didn't share my enthusiasm, but she saw a benefit: she could wear her makeup. As it turned out, it was small consolation.

We stayed in a small bungalow with open windows protected by steel bars to keep wild animals out. On one side of the little building was a bed with mosquito netting. The bathroom was on the other side, though we quickly learned that various cultures had different ideas about bathrooms. There was a hole in the concrete floor. To this day I can still see the look of horror on Marja's face when I told her the purpose of the hole in the floor. America had been a big adjustment for her, and now, in a very short time, she was in a totally foreign culture with her brand-new husband.

Most of the people in the village had never seen a blonde-haired person before, and they stared at Marja like she was a goddess. The women and little girls were especially fascinated. She wanted to be kind to them, so she invited them into the hunting compound and showed them her clothes. A little girl stared at one of Marja's negligees, so Marja gave it to her. She was thrilled. In fact, she was so excited that at a festival a couple of days later, the little girl wore the negligee for everyone to see. It was quite a sight!

On the first morning of our hunt, our guide gave us firm instructions before taking us out into the bush: "If you shoot a tiger, stay in the oxcart," he warned. "Don't jump out. Stay in the cart and shoot him several times. They are very strong, and even after taking several bullets, they can charge and kill you."

I glanced at Marja. She looked like she was going to be sick, but that would come later. We piled into the wooden cart that was harnessed to two unenthusiastic oxen. After the guide barked out a loud command, the oxen began lumbering down a bumpy path into the jungle. Perhaps noticing our discomfort as we bounced along in the rough-hewn wooden cart, our guide explained that they hunted this way because we could get closer to our quarry. Tigers and other beasts weren't afraid of oxen, and sometimes tigers welcomed them as meals. It occurred to me that getting so close to a tiger might not be a great idea. That day, we didn't see a tiger, but I was able to shoot a sambar, which is a large elk-like animal with huge antlers and a heavy coat of fur. I was excited, but Marja was livid. She knew that the purpose of our hunt was to bring back an animal that would provide food for the villagers, but seeing the magnificent animal fall to the ground was more than she could take. Unfortunately, the shot didn't kill the sambar, so according to Muslim custom, we had to slit its throat, which produced the most pathetic bellowing I've ever heard. To add insult to injury, Marja had to ride all the way back to the compound sitting on top of the dead beast. She wasn't happy.

As the sun dipped beneath the horizon, our guide yanked on the reins and motioned for us to keep still. In an instant, he pointed into the trees. There, crouched low to the ground was a Bengal tiger, at the time both prized and legal to hunt. Slowly, the guide handed me a Rigby .470—an elephant gun that packed such a wallop I had been warned not to shoot it in the prone position because it would break my collarbone. I carefully stood up in the oxcart and shouldered the double-barreled gun . . . then squeezed the trigger. Even over the blast of the gun, we could hear the tiger roar. In the dusk it appeared to have fallen dead to the ground. Completely forgetting the guide's warning, I jumped from the cart and walked toward the groaning beast, ready to fire the other round in the chamber. Suddenly, the wounded tiger

MY PRIZED SAMBAR BEING PREPARED BY VILLAGERS FOR THE FEAST

jumped to its feet and, fortunately for me, limped off into the bush. I didn't have time for a second shot. Conscientious hunters know that you never leave a wounded animal to die, so we followed the tiger's trail deeper into the forest. We knew that at any second, it could pounce from the shadows. Finally, it got too dark and dangerous to continue, so we walked back to the cart.

We left the next day. Later we learned that local trackers found the tiger when the vultures circled the dead carcass. The missionary was kind enough to ship its hide back to our home in the United States, but our experiences on the hunt and the beautiful tiger skin failed to make a good impression on Marja. In her first weeks as my wife, it was becoming clear to both of us that beginning our journey together under these conditions wasn't working very well. Every day in the Philippines, the missionary's wife complained to me about the way Marja dressed, especially about her makeup. Instead of defending her,

I asked Marja to remove her makeup before every service. Then in India, trekking through the jungles and having to stay in the primitive bungalow only made things worse. We'd only been married a very short time, and already the strain on our relationship was palpable. First, ours was a cross-cultural marriage, something a bit unusual in those days in my world of evangelists and pastors. We had few resources to help us understand what we didn't know about each other. Second, it wasn't a question of love—we genuinely loved each other, but in looking back, we probably rushed into things too quickly. Marja was a new believer, from another country, and she married an evangelist. And a honeymoon tiger hunt? That's a recipe for disaster. The strain in our relationship was showing. I knew I had to do something about it.

Our plan had been to continue traveling around the world holding crusades. Some of the largest and most influential churches in many different countries had invited me to hold revivals. I had thought this would be a great opportunity for Marja to see the world—it was a trip of a lifetime—but instead, she was very unhappy and homesick for her parents. I realized that I needed to pay more attention to her needs, so I canceled the remaining revivals in Asia and Europe and bought two tickets to Sweden.

In Sweden—one of the coldest places on the planet in December—we enjoyed a wonderful time with Marja's parents. We had decided to get married so quickly that they were unable to attend our wedding, so I was meeting them for the first time. Her dad, a wonderful man who was the fire chief in the community, was an atheist, but it didn't seem to bother him that his daughter had married a Christian preacher. We were only there for a couple of weeks, but it was just what Marja needed. I knew I had made the right decision.

From there we flew to Sacramento, California, where I led a revival in the largest Assembly of God church at the time. Its pastor,

Clyde Henson, was a famous rodeo rider who had found the Lord and felt called to the ministry. I inspected Marja every night before the services, and if she had makeup on, I asked her to wipe it off. She did . . . reluctantly. As soon as each service was over, she rushed back to where we were staying and put her makeup back on. It dawned on me that many of the rules for the wife of an evangelist are unfair. For example, I could dress as sharply as I wanted, slick my hair back in the latest style, and look really cool, but our wives had to look dour and old-fashioned. To be honest, I didn't really believe in those crazy expectations, but I knew that if I wanted to lead a revival, I'd have to make sure my wife met the crowd's expectations. It was a real struggle for both of us, and I wish I had handled it far better.

The joy we experienced in Sweden quickly faded as the stark reality of what it would take for her to be married to a prominent evangelist began to sink in. Despite the undercurrent of disappointment and bitterness that had crept into our marriage, the Holy Spirit moved in a mighty way during the revival In Sacramento. We sometimes think we have to be perfect in order to be used by the Lord, but we only need to be willing. His Spirit overpowers all our human hindrances and draws the lost to His side.

For the next few weeks, we held more revivals. Marja and I fought over her makeup and dresses during the day, and we watched miraculous outpourings of the Holy Spirit each night. I couldn't see it at the time, but Marja was a loyal and dedicated wife who did her best to support me in my ministry. She was as passionate about seeing people saved as I was. In fact, when I gave an altar call, she often went to the altar with all the others who wanted to be saved—not because she didn't think she was right with the Lord, but because she wanted to be there for me. How do you honor that kind of commitment from a woman who was distraught over her role yet so willing to accept it?

I had the answer to that question. I made one of the most difficult decisions of my life.

DIFFICULT TIMES AHEAD

CHAPTER 14

The Right Decision Followed by a Crisis

Before and after marrying Marja, I was at the peak of my ministry as an evangelist. For some reason, in God's perfect timing, He chose to bless my ministry beyond my wildest imagination. I could barely keep up with the demand as pastors from all over America invited me to preach at their revivals and conferences. Sometimes the altar calls would go on for thirty minutes as scores of people came forward to turn their lives over to God and be filled with the Holy Spirit. But I knew if I kept going, I'd lose Marja.

We had shared our struggles with my parents, and they suggested we take a couple of years off. "Why don't you move back to Kansas City?" my dad offered. "You can get a job and help out at the church."

My friends in ministry thought I was crazy to leave when God was blessing us in such wonderful ways, but I had to follow God's clear leading. We drove to Kansas City and bought a large old house. We didn't own a single piece of furniture, but people from my dad's church brought things over: a bed, a kitchen table, a couple of overstuffed chairs, and lots more. By her own admission, Marja was inexperienced in the kitchen, but she knew how to make Swedish pancakes. Guess what we ate at almost every meal? But even as we began this new phase of our lives and added little touches to make our house our own, Marja remained unhappy. I thought she just needed some time to experience relief from the stress of being an evangelist's wife. Even though I would be helping my dad at the church, he couldn't pay me much, and I had to find a way to support us.

I heard that a tree-trimming company was looking for workers, so I drove across town to their office and asked for an application. I must have looked out of place because the guy in charge asked me if I'd ever trimmed trees before.

"No, sir," I responded. "But I'm not afraid of hard work, and I can learn."

I got the job, but it was only part-time, so I found another part-time job working at an auto supply store. Every morning I got up early to trim trees, then after eating a sack lunch, I drove to the auto supply store. Every Sunday night I preached the evening evangelistic service at my dad's church.

It was more than a little humbling to go from being one of the leading evangelists in the United States to trimming trees and selling spark plugs. However, the Lord used this time to teach me about how people—the ones who came to my revivals and eventually to the churches I would pastor—really lived. It's easy for people in ministry to become isolated and insulated from the people they want to serve. My two jobs weren't very inspiring, but I gave them my best every day, believing that this two-year break would help Marja and me.

One morning I bounded down the stairs, ready to head out for another day of work. I was proud that we had our own home and I was able to earn enough for us to live comfortably. Things seemed to be going well. I grabbed my lunch from the kitchen counter, and when I walked into the little living room, I saw Marja standing at the front door. She was holding a suitcase.

"Tommy, I'm leaving you today."

I couldn't believe what I was hearing. "Why?"

With tears running down her cheeks, she told me, "I'm hindering you, Tommy. God called you to serve Him as an evangelist, and I'm an obstacle. I'm holding you back from doing what you love—from doing what God called you to do. I just can't be a good preacher's wife."

I tried to reassure her, "Oh, honey, you're doing a great job. People love you. Everything's going to be fine."

But she had made her mind up, and no matter how much I begged and pleaded, she just shook her head. "No, Tommy, I've got to leave. I'm sorry."

She asked me to drive her to the airport. It was one of the longest and quietest rides I've ever had. When we pulled into the short-term parking lot, I asked her one more time to stay, but she just looked down and shook her head.

We got out of the car. I went inside to help her check her bag, and then we walked to her gate. Soon they called for all passengers to board, and all I could do was watch her walk down the jetway. I stood by the window and waited as the baggage handlers loaded the last suitcases into the plane. Then the jetway slowly pulled back, and the tractor pushed the jet onto the tarmac. I watched the plane all the way down the taxiway until it stood at the end of the runway. Moments later, it began moving, slowly, but it picked up speed until the nose gently lifted. The engines roared as the plane climbed into the bright blue sky.

And then it was gone. She was gone.

I HATED TO SEE THE PLANE TAKE OFF

And so were all my dreams. It was over. I loved Marja, and I wanted to spend the rest of my life with her, but she was gone. I felt unbearably empty. But there was another consequence of her leaving me: In those days, you couldn't be divorced and serve in ministry, and even if you could, I didn't want a divorce. Going it alone was out of the question. I stood staring out the window for a long, long time. I had no idea what to do. Marja was on her way back to California where she had made some friends before we met. I was standing in an airport . . . utterly devastated and alone. It was the saddest day of my life.

Finally, I walked to the parking lot in a daze and drove to our house. I began praying, crying, and wondering out loud, "What am

I going to do?" All I had ever wanted to do since I was a little boy was to preach the gospel, and in an instant, that dream was gone. I didn't blame Marja. I knew she tried her best to fit in and support my ministry. It made me love her even more—though it broke my heart—to hear her say she was leaving because she thought she was preventing me from fulfilling my calling. She knew that it was because of her that I was trimming trees instead of preaching to thousands. The more I thought about what had just happened, the more I cried out to God, "What am I going to do? Where will I go? What's going to happen now?" The minutes in that lonely house stretched into hours. In the evening, the growing darkness mirrored my troubled soul.

My mind was racing to find an answer, but it was late, and I knew I needed to try and get some sleep. I still had to get up and trim trees the next morning, and somehow, find a way to explain to my mom and dad that Marja had left me. I knew they would be compassionate and supportive, but I still dreaded telling them. In what seemed like the proverbial "blink of an eye," my entire life had been turned upside down, and it felt horrible. As I headed upstairs to our bedroom, the phone rang. It was Marja!

"Oh, Tommy," she began in her broken English. "I think I've made a terrible mistake. Could you find it in your heart to forgive me and let me come back home?"

"Of course!" I shouted into the phone as we both cried. I told her how much I loved her and missed her and couldn't wait to see her again.

"Are you sure, Tommy?"

"Absolutely! Just buy a ticket for the first flight home."

The next day I sped back to the airport, only this time my heart was filled with unbelievable joy. My wife was on her way home! I arrived at the airport two hours early. I parked the car and raced to her gate carrying a huge bouquet of roses. I nervously paced back and forth for what seemed like forever until I finally heard a voice over the P.A. system: "United flight 296 from Los Angeles is now arriving at Gate 63." Minutes later the door to the jetway opened. As the first passengers appeared, I peered over their heads, standing on my tip-toes to look for Marja. Then I saw her! My heart jumped, and maybe I did, too. My dear Marja was back! I pushed my way to the entrance, and when she walked through it, I gave her a big hug, handed her the roses, and smiled, "Welcome home, honey!"

When we got to the car, we joined hands and prayed: "Oh, God. We're going to make this work. We're going to do it for better for worse. For richer or poorer. In sickness and in health." We made a commitment in the car that we weren't going to quit, no matter what. Yes, we had taken those vows at our wedding, but I think it took this emotional trauma to get our attention and show us that we could weather any storm.

It would have been easier to give up, but as I look back at all that God has accomplished through us over the years, I'm so glad we didn't. If we had quit, there wouldn't have been a Matthew and a Dream Center. There wouldn't have been a Luke, and the Dream City Church. If we had have quit, there couldn't have been a Kristie, who God has used to reach and stir the hearts of women around the world.

We drove home as happy as newlyweds. I got up the next morning and went to work. I came home every night to a beautiful woman. Both of us knew we were right where God wanted us to be. We settled into an ordinary routine and awaited what God had for us next. He soon showed us.

THE FIRST CHURCH I PASTORED IN
DAVENPORT, IOWA, 1971

CHAPTER 15

A Church in My Heart

I loved being an evangelist, but it wasn't my ultimate goal. From my first summer preaching at revivals, I believed my work as an evangelist was a way to prepare to pastor a church. That's what I really felt called to do, but I knew I wasn't ready, especially at the age of seventeen. During my years as an evangelist, I studied hard to understand each passage I was preaching. In addition, I became a student of churches. I kept a notebook with a list of the things I thought churches did right—things I hoped to do when I became a pastor. Then I made another list—church practices that didn't seem to work well. I pledged to avoid doing those when I became a pastor.

I loved preaching and cared deeply about every person who came forward, and during all those years, I was building a church in my heart. I was creating a vision of what can be. I observed the way they took an offering, welcomed people into the church, selected the music, gave an altar call, and followed up with visitors. As I drove from revival to revival, I was beginning to catch a vision for the kind of pastor I wanted to be and the kind of church I wanted to lead. My evangelistic work was helpful because the church I would eventually pastor would focus on introducing people to Jesus as their Savior. To be honest, I was pretty sure I knew what kind of church I wanted to pastor.

When I was a boy, the great evangelist and pastor, Charles Fuller, came to Kansas City, and my dad took me every night to hear him preach. Fuller was one of the first pastors to broadcast his services over radio. His *Old Fashioned Revival Hour* was carried on the ABC radio network and was heard on more than 650 radio stations across the nation with a combined audience of more than ten million. The demands of his radio ministry became so great that he resigned from the pastorate, devoting full time to his broadcasts and holding revivals. In 1947 he founded Fuller Theological Seminary in Pasadena, California, which is one of the largest and most influential seminaries in the world.

As he did in every city, Fuller rented the largest auditorium in town, and every night it was packed. More than 7,000 people filled the place as Fuller's famous pianist, Rudy Atwood, accompanied a huge choir from churches all over Kansas City. I was transfixed by his preaching. On the last night of the revival, I leaned over to my dad and said, "Someday I'm going to pastor a church this big."

My dad was a wise man. He could have dismissed such childish ambition with a laugh or told me that I was dreaming too big. At the time, there wasn't a church in the entire world that big. He told me, "Son, I believe you can do it if you humble yourself, keep your eyes on the Lord, love God, and live a good life. Keep your motives right and your life clean, and I believe God can use you to build that kind of church." My dad believed in me, and more importantly, he believed in the God who lived in me.

Over the years I've had a lot of people share a dream they felt God had given them. Some were real whoppers, but I learned from my dad never to discourage anyone from doing what they thought God was calling them to do. Our job is to encourage people and let God take care of the results. I suspected that many of those who shared their dreams with me would never make it, and some of the ones I was sure would accomplish their dreams never did, but God has fulfilled the dreams of some far beyond what they had envisioned. We don't decide who God's going to bless. My dad was the voice of encouragement that said, "Go for it!"

I eventually quit my tree-trimming and auto parts jobs and returned to evangelistic work. Although Marja still felt a bit out of place among church people, she was a real trooper. She was committed to being by my side through thick and thin, comfort and awkwardness, makeup or no makeup. I'm sorry to say that some pastors' wives didn't treat her warmly. In spite of that, we were determined to make our marriage work, and every day we grew closer and closer.

One night at a revival in St. Louis, Missouri, Marja suddenly got up and rushed out of the service. I saw her leave, but I had no idea what had happened. After the service, I asked her if everything was all right. She told me she had experienced a sudden wave of nausea and didn't want to get sick in the church. I knew exactly what her problem was. The next night, without consulting a doctor, I announced to the entire church that we were going to have a baby! I think Marja was as shocked as everyone else by my announcement, but I was certain that she was pregnant. I was thrilled because I wanted so much to be a father.

A few days later, she had an appointment with a doctor, and he confirmed my diagnosis. Eight months later, after a harrowing ride to the hospital complicated by a flat tire and complete with a police escort, she gave birth to Kristie, a beautiful baby girl. Thirteen months later, Kristie got a little brother, Luke.

That's when I decided it was time to follow my dream to become a pastor. When I was traveling as an evangelist, I didn't feel right about leaving Marja at home with two kids—sometimes for weeks at a time—so I let it be known to some of the larger churches looking for pastors that I was available. I had prayed about it and felt God was calling me to serve Him in this way.

Not a single large church responded.

After a few weeks, I put my name out to all the medium-sized churches looking for a pastor. I was certain they were waiting just for me, and they might even fight over me, because after all, I was such a successful evangelist.

Not a single medium-sized church responded.

Undaunted, but getting a little impatient, I sent my name around to dozens of little churches. Surely these churches would love to have a big-time evangelist come and pastor their church!

None of them wanted me either.

Finally, I got on my knees and prayed, "God, whatever door you open, I'll step through it. I don't care where it is or what size it is, I'll go." This utter dependence is exactly where God wanted me! A couple of days later, I got a call from Westside Assemblies of God, a little church in Davenport, Iowa. They asked if I'd I come for a "tryout," which was a chance for them to meet me, hear me preach, interview me, and then decide if they wanted me . . . or not. We settled on a date. I was excited to finally get the chance to become a pastor.

At the time, many people considered Davenport a sleepy little river town, but I considered it the garden spot of America. My optimism is rooted in my belief that God can work wonders anywhere and everywhere. I've always felt that way. I believe your attitude can make experiences either wonderful or awful, and I've always chosen to see the good in everything and everyone. I thought my kids were the best looking and smartest, and my wife is the most beautiful woman in the world. My dog could bark louder than anyone else's dog, and the skunk in my neighborhood is the biggest stinker. That's just the way I am. The grass is always greener on my side of the fence, not the other side like most people assume.

My enthusiasm about going to Davenport proved to be a bit premature because when I arrived at the little church, I was introduced to 76 of the meanest Christians you'll ever find! The men were stern and fierce—I don't remember seeing a single one of them smile. The ladies wore dresses down to their ankles, and their expressions were just as forbidding. Thankfully, Marja—who was sick at the time—didn't come with me to meet the congregation. They would have scared her to death . . . or she would have scared *them* to death.

The church was a small wood-framed building that seated about seventy people. If everyone came, they wouldn't all fit. When you walked through the front door, a narrow stairway to the left took you down to the basement, which was dark and foreboding. The sanctuary held six rows of worn wooden pews, and a few bare light bulbs hung from wires attached to the low ceiling. The church had an antiquated upright piano, and whatever the pianist played sounded like "The Old Rugged Cross." The song leader was a deacon who couldn't sing. He just stood behind the pulpit and moved the hymnal up and down.

That's the bad news . . . or at least most of it. The good news was that the church had bought a piece of property in the industrial district and was building a new facility. It was a low-roofed building with fake brick walls. This one had a plastic steeple they'd bought through mail order. Unfortunately, they had run out of money, so I would have to begin raising funds immediately to finish the construction. The church leaders informed me that their offerings barely covered their expenses, but they could pay me a percentage of any surplus . . . if they got any. The total income for that year was $25,000. Who could pass up an offer like that?

After a quick assessment of the situation, I made up my mind to refuse their call even if I passed the test, but I still had to preach the

Sunday morning and evening services. Most candidates for a pastor-ate preach the kind of sermon that wouldn't offend anyone: sermons about how good God is or the blessings of being a Christian. I didn't want to be offered the job and then turn them down, so I decided to bring the fire with both barrels! On Sunday morning, I delivered a strong and convicting salvation message to these unforgiving saints and, amazingly, three came forward to get saved! The deacons later told me they hadn't seen anyone find the Lord there in years.

I honestly didn't want them to offer me the job, so that night I preached one of my strongest sermons: "Can a Man Rob God?" This message wasn't about money; it was about people who claim to be Christians but never give God the praise and glory due Him, robbing God of the joy of blessing them. I thought this sermon would surely scare them off, but again, people streamed to the altar. As I was pray-ing at the altar with those who had come forward, a group of men exited to a small room to the side of the platform.

After the altar service, everyone returned to their seats for the benediction, but the head of the deacons approached the pulpit. He announced, "Ladies and gentlemen, the board just met, and we have elected Pastor Barnett to be our new pastor!"

I couldn't believe my ears. I had just preached two of my stron-gest hellfire-and-brimstone sermons, but they still wanted me to be their pastor. At that point, I didn't have the heart to turn them down. I thanked them, got in my car, and prayed for six hours, all the way home to Kansas City, "God, what am I going to do?" As much as I wanted to be a pastor, I didn't want to go to that church. But how could I get out of it?

As always when I'm faced with a difficult issue, I went to my dad. I told him the whole story and that I didn't want to accept their offer. He thought for a minute and then said, "Well, son, here's what you do. Call them and thank them for being so gracious to you. Tell them how much you enjoyed meeting with them but that you've prayed about it, and you just don't feel that this is what God wants you to do."

I told him I couldn't do that because they were so nice to me and they believed it was God's will. I asked him if he would do it for me. He shook his head and grumbled, "You haven't got enough backbone to be a pastor," but he agreed to call the head deacon, Otto Winkler, and get me out of my dilemma.

Dad told him, "Otto, my son wanted me to call you and tell you he loves you and all the good people of your church, but he prayed about it, and he just doesn't feel it's where God wants him to go right now. Besides, I need him here at the church to keep helping me, so we're asking respectfully that you release him."

THE DEDICATION OF OUR NEW BUILDING IN DAVENPORT, IOWA, IN 1975

Otto, a German immigrant like most of the church members, was direct in his answer: "I'm afraid we can't do that. We have an agreement."

Dad told me about the conversation. At that point, I realized I had to go. I remembered I had prayed and told God that I'd go through any door He opened for me, and He had opened this door. Marja and I sold our house and packed up our things. On a Saturday we drove six hours to Davenport. I would begin my ministry the following day.

As we drove up U.S. 136 toward Davenport, I knew I had to have a difficult conversation with Marja. "Honey, you know the battles we've had about your makeup?" I glanced at her, and she gave me "that look," but I continued, "Well, these people are pretty conservative, so could you please pick out the plainest dress you have for church tomorrow so we can make a good impression?"

Marja didn't say a word, but the next morning she came downstairs in a plain white knit dress and pulled her lovely blonde hair back in a bun and, of course, she didn't wear any makeup. When she walked into church with me that first Sunday, you could almost hear an audible gasp. They'd never seen anyone as beautiful as Marja.

She was just one of the changes this little congregation would be facing with their new pastor.

DAVENPORT'S EASTER EGG HUNT,
OVER 3,000 ATTENDED 1977

**TAKING A COMMUNITY FOR CHRIST:
FROM A SUNDAY SCHOOL OF 76 TO
MORE THAN 2000 IN FOUR YEARS**

the Westside Story

Charles R.
Hembree

OUR FIRST BOOK AT WESTSIDE ASSEMBLY,
DAVENPORT

CHAPTER 16

Old Buses, New Believers

I've never agreed with the church "experts" who advise pastors who have just come to a church to tread lightly so they could gradually bring the congregation around to their new ideas and new programs. There's a different method I prefer: Go in and shoot all your big guns, let everyone know exactly where you're going, and most importantly, start leading people to Christ. You're probably going to lose some people who don't want anything to change, but that's fine. You'll replace them with people eager to join you in your mission. Old wineskins can't hold new wine. I hate to say this, but a lot of church people don't really want new people coming in. They feel threatened (or at least uncomfortable) around people they don't know, especially if those people don't look like them.

In Davenport, we had to do something immediately to let people know what kind of church God wanted to build. The most important word in that sentence is "we." I assumed they had called me because they wanted to do big things for God at Westside Assemblies of God.

My dad had given me an old International Harvester school bus that he didn't dare use anymore. The engine barely ran, and when it did, it was hard to keep the bus going straight because its steering was so bad. I named our bus "She Needs": she needed tires, she needed gas, she needed a paint job, she needed a complete overhaul. I wasn't sure what I would do with it, so I just parked it out behind the church.

On my second Sunday as pastor, a lady introduced herself and shared something that caught my attention. "Pastor, I've been saved for only a few months, and I don't know if I'm supposed to do this, but I've been going out every week knocking on doors in my neighborhood leading people to Christ. I've got so many of them now, but I don't know how to get them to church because a lot of them don't have cars. When I told some of the people at church about it, they told me just to let them find their own church. I don't want to make anyone angry, but I'd sure like to get them involved in our church."

I couldn't believe my ears. I told her, "Sister, you're exactly who I'm looking for. I'm going to give you a bus!"

The lady, her husband, and I walked behind the church and got into that dilapidated old bus. I got it started and showed her how to put it in gear. Then I had her drive it around the block. I confess that I was a little nervous as she worked that stubborn clutch and jerked forward every time we started into an intersection. She didn't mind that the bus was a dinosaur—she literally beamed as she sat behind the wheel. She was a tiny lady, barely tall enough to see over the steering wheel.

On the first Sunday of our new bus ministry, she picked up more than sixty people and brought them to church. The bus only held forty-eight, so many of them had to stand in the aisle. You should have seen the looks on the faces of the regular attenders as those sixty strangers marched into our little church and found a place to sit. I preached to a standing-room-only audience, and when I gave the altar call, twenty of the bus riders came forward and accepted Christ. I was thrilled, but I was in the minority. We lost a few families that Sunday. I never like losing anyone, but God has called us to fulfill the Great Commission and win the lost, no matter the cost.

A young deacon and his wife approached me after church that day. They understood what had happened. The deacon said, "Pastor, I'm so happy that we're reaching out to the lost. I'll tell you what I'm going to do. I'm going to buy you another bus!"

I told the deacon, "That's great, but who's going to drive it?"

He and his wife looked at each other and shrugged their shoulders. He turned to me and smiled, "Well, I guess we could."

He bought another old bus. It turned out to be another She Needs. We called it "He Needs." In less than two weeks, *that* bus was full. By now, we had moved into our new building, and soon we bought a third bus. Then another. And another. We kept buying more buses, picking up more people who needed Jesus, and rejoicing when they accepted Christ. The only way we could accommodate all these new people was to have several services every Sunday.

During the first year at Davenport, I held a revival at a church in St. Petersburg, Florida, where Bill Wilson, the children's pastor, approached me and asked if I could teach him how to run a bus ministry. His church had bought an old bus and wanted him to use it to pick up kids for their Vacation Bible School. He thought it could also be used to start a bus ministry for Sunday school kids, but he didn't know where to begin. I explained how he needed to have an adult on board—a bus pastor—to watch over the kids and follow up with "the fifteen-second call." The plan is to drive around on Saturday, knock on the door of each child on his bus route, and when the parent comes to the door, simply say, "Hi, I'm Bill, Bobby's bus pastor. I want to make sure he'll be ready for the bus tomorrow morning." A quick thank-you ends the conversation, all of which takes only about fifteen seconds,

OUR BUS DIRECTOR, BILL WILSON

and then go to the next house. This way we're not only showing that we care about their children, but we're also making a connection with the parents, who we hope one day will join little Bobby at our church. Bill hung on every word and followed me around the whole week of the revival. He was eager to do great things for the Lord.

Not long after the revival, I got a call from Bill telling me that their senior pastor had unexpectedly died, adding, "We're up to ten buses now, and it looks like my work is done here. Could I come to Davenport and be your bus pastor?"

I was impressed by his heart for ministry and how quickly he grew the bus ministry in an otherwise struggling church. I answered, "Sure, Bill. I'd love to have you join us!"

By the time I left the church in Davenport—are you ready for this?—we had forty-seven buses picking people up all over the city and in areas outside of town. These were people who, for whatever reason, didn't have a church of their own. Bill's vision was even bigger. After I left Davenport for Phoenix, he went to New York City and started a new ministry for kids. He called it Metro Ministries (now Metro World Child), and today it serves 250,000 at-risk children worldwide every week.

Many of the people the buses brought to church were kids, and not everyone was happy about that. Some people grumbled that all we were doing was providing a couple of hours of free babysitting, but it just made sense to me. When you reach kids, you're dealing with the closest thing to their parents' hearts. The parents of the kids we brought to church almost always followed the kids, and many accepted Christ.

Sometimes we forget that the church is for the lost. Jesus said, "It's not the healthy who need a doctor, but the sick. I have not come to call the righteous but sinners" (Mark 2:17 NIV). When I use the term "lost," I don't mean it as an insult. I love the lost. Apart from the forgiveness Christ offers, every person is lost. Every Christian should love the lost and invite them to church so they, too, can experience the cleansing of the cross and be transformed by the power of the Holy Spirit. I've said it often, but I'll do anything in good taste to get the lost to come to church. The method isn't sacred; the message is. In our church, not everyone shared my idea of good taste.

For example, one Easter we decided to have a huge Easter egg hunt to get kids to come to Sunday school. By this time I had learned how to use the media to get free publicity, and the newspapers and local television stations announced that families could take their kids to a free Easter egg hunt at our church. We were ready for them. We had thousands of colored hard-boiled eggs, candy eggs, and plastic eggs filled with prizes—candy or little toys. I decided to offer a special bo-nus. I bought a bunch of little chicks only a few days old. In those days you could buy ones that were dyed bright colors. I had all the baby chicks in a big pen behind the church, and early Sunday morning, we handed out the plastic eggs. Some of the eggs contained tickets for one of the chicks.

About three thousand kids came, and you should have seen the looks on their faces when they opened up an egg and got a ticket for a chick! The kids loved it, the parents loved it, and the media loved it . . . and that's where my problems started.

On Monday morning, I heard a loud knock on our parsonage door. I opened it to a not-too-pleasant looking lady who said she was from the Humane Society. She didn't bother with introductions. "Reverend Barnett, what you did with those chickens is against the law!"

I explained, "Ma'am, I had no idea it was illegal. I used to raise chickens when I was younger. All we were doing was giving away a few little chicks to our Sunday school kids."

She wasn't buying my reasoning: "It doesn't matter if you knew it was legal or not, it's against the law. I could have you arrested and thrown in jail right this minute."

That scared me. "Well, ma'am, I'm really sorry. I didn't mean any harm, and as far as I know, none of those baby chicks was hurt. I promise I'll never do that again."

My contrition and promise seemed to satisfy her, and she said she would let it go this time. She started walking to her car. For some reason, something came over me. I told her, "Ma'am, before you leave I need to confess something." That got her attention, and she turned around. I continued, "I gave away baby chickens, but I ate their mom-mas." She didn't appreciate my attempt at humor.

I always looked for ways to get more people to come to church and find Jesus, and this commitment created yet another problem, but this time, a good one: we kept running out of room. We needed more space, but we didn't have much money because we reached a lot of poor people—single moms, families hit hard by unemployment, and people in disadvantaged neighborhoods. These people did their best to give from their meager resources, but it's difficult to build new buildings that way. Still, God provided: over an eight-year period, we built four new buildings, all without a contractor.

Every day during the construction process, I drove to the church and handled my responsibilities as pastor. I only had one staff member—a secretary. I was the preacher, the music director, the treasurer, the bus ministry director, the children's church preacher, and the pastor who called on people in the hospital. All my years as an evangelist and working as an assistant to my father taught me how to fulfill all these roles. I had developed a strong work ethic, and I knew it took a lot of work to build a strong church.

At 5 o'clock every day, I drove home to Marja and, with the arrival of Matthew, our three children. We ate supper, listened to each of the kids tell me about their day at school, and then I drove back to the church where I joined several other men of the church as we poured concrete, framed in the buildings, put roofs on them, laid bricks, and did all the finish work inside, including plumbing and electricity. It was the only way we could grow because we didn't have enough money to pay professionals.

First, we built the new church building, then a bus garage, then, when we outgrew our church, we built a much bigger building, about 250 feet long. The first two-thirds was our sanctuary that held around 1,500 people, and the rest was a gym we used for the children's ministry. When this space proved too small for our kids, we built a 40,000 square foot building for our children's church. Every night for eight years, I drove back to the church and worked with men who were volunteering to build the new buildings.

One night at the supper table, Luke eagerly asked, "Dad, can you stay home tonight?"

The boys were young—Luke was probably eight or nine and Matthew was five or six. I answered him, "I'd love to, Luke, but I've got to meet with the building committee tonight because we're going over plans for the new church. I'd much rather stay here with you, but I really have to go."

"Can Matthew and I go with you?"

I was amused, but I asked him, "It may be a long meeting. What would you do all that time?"

He had an answer: "We could go to the gym and play basketball. It'll be great. We just want to be with you."

That broke my heart. I said, "Sure, the two of you can come." After supper, we hopped in the car and drove to the church, both boys talking my ears off all the way. When we got there, they ran to the gym, and I went to my office to meet with the building committee. To be honest, I forgot all about the boys as we looked over plans, made adjustments, and set up a work schedule. It was after ten o'clock before we were done. Suddenly I remembered the boys. When I opened the door, I saw them on the floor, sound asleep next to the door, using choir robes as blankets. They had gotten as close to their dad as possible.

I carried each boy to the car. I put Matthew in the back seat and Luke in the front. Matthew was sound asleep, but Luke woke up enough to put his head on my leg. All the way home I prayed, "Oh God, help me. I don't want to miss these moments! I want to carry out the Great Commission, but I don't want to lose my children."

When we got home, I put Matthew in bed, then went back out to the car and carried Luke up to his bed. When I pulled the covers back to tuck him in, he suddenly opened his big, beautiful blue eyes, looked up at me and said, "Daddy, this has been the nicest night ever. I'd rather be with you than anybody in all the world. Thank you, Daddy, for letting us come along with you tonight."

I tried to hold back my tears as I answered, "Son, the reason I'm away so much is not because I don't want to be with you, but because I want you to have the kind of world I enjoyed when I was growing up. I want you to live in a country where you're free to play sports and enjoy all the good in our land. I'm just doing my part by trying to build a church that will be a model for other churches so that people will see the good works and glorify God."

Then, kneeling beside his bed, I began to pray: "God, I've given my time, I've given my money, I've given everything to You. But there's one thing I've never given to You, and that's my children. And tonight, I give Kristie, Luke, and Matthew to You . . ."

Before I said "amen," Luke interrupted me and started praying: "Dear God, You know how much I love my daddy. I'd rather be with him than anybody in all the world. But tonight, my daddy has given me to You. And now, God, I give my daddy to You."

That was a major turning point in my life and my ministry. In that precious moment, I understood that God didn't expect me to lose my family as I served Him. From that point on, even though we still had a lot of work to do to finish building the church, I found ways to spend more time with my kids. I began taking them with me on hospital calls, and I carved out time for them on Saturdays.

Ministry is important, but I don't believe God expects people to sacrifice their families to serve Him. I've seen many tragic examples of that happening, and I'm grateful that I learned fairly early to avoid the same well-intentioned mistake. Another thing I learned was that my church didn't suffer at all from my decision to spend more time with my family. They fully supported me, and we never missed a beat.

I still had plenty of innovative ways of getting people to church.

EATING PART OF OUR GIANT WORLD-RECORD POPSICLE, AS REPORTED BY GUINNESS BOOK OF WORLD RECORDS

CHAPTER 17

Popsicles and Porn

By the end of my first year at Davenport, we were averaging 500 in attendance, and at the end of our second year, we were over 1000. We kept growing until we hit 4,000, making us one of the first megachurches in the evangelical world.

While I was a pastor in Davenport, Iowa's United States Senator, Roger Jepsen, found Christ and was filled with the Holy Spirit in our church. The county sheriff and other prominent leaders in our city got saved and regularly attended our church, but so did a lot of people no one ever heard of because I still followed my dad's advice: go after the people nobody else wants.

For example, Bill Wilson believed we could draw a lot of new children to Sunday school by making the world's biggest popsicle. I thought it was a great idea. Bill took some men to the local ice plant and asked the manager to create a huge block of ice flavored with lime. By huge, I mean eight feet tall and four feet wide. For popsicle sticks, we used two 4" x 4" posts usually used to build pole barns. That was the easy part. We had a big logistical problem: How do you move a 6,000-pound lime-green popsicle from the ice plant to our church? Our solution became a phenomenal marketing strategy—we hired a mobile crane to go to the icehouse, lift it in a special sling, and then slowly rumble down the streets to our church. Can you imagine playing in your front yard and seeing a giant popsicle slowly moving past your house? By the time the crane got to the church and set the posts into holes we'd dug, the lawn was filled with kids. We began chipping off pieces and handing it to them so they could say they ate from the world's biggest popsicle. I was thrilled that our popsicle made it into *the Guinness Book of World Records*. (Actually, this was the second of these awards for our family. My dad made it into that same record book for playing the longest handball game in history.)

The popsicle brought a lot of new kids to church, but it provided another unexpected result. That day a man showed up after church to pick up his daughter, and he'd been drinking heavily the night before. He took one look at the melting popsicle and blinked, wondering if he was seeing things. A few weeks later, he came to church and got saved. He told one of our men, "When I saw that big thing on the church lawn, I swore I wasn't going to drink anymore as long as I live!"

The popsicle worked so well that the next summer we decided to build the world's biggest banana split. We got more than a hundred yards of rain gutters, and while the kids were in Sunday school, volunteers filled them with ice cream, piled on the bananas, poured chocolate syrup over everything, and sprinkled it with peanuts. As soon as Sunday school was over, the kids grabbed plastic spoons, ran to the banana split, and devoured it. As it turned out, it was a colossal mess—in the summer heat, all the ice cream melted. Do you think that stopped the kids? Instead of using the spoons, they got down on all fours and slurped it all up. If the health department had seen what happened, I'd probably still be in jail.

PART OF THE ARMY DISPLAY ON STAND UP
FOR AMERICA SUNDAY, 1975

Not all my ideas for getting people in church were as crazy as those. While I was at Davenport, young people all over America were protesting the war in Vietnam. I respect the right of anyone who wants to peacefully protest, but these protesters were burning the American flag and showing disrespect for our country. Our brave soldiers returning from the battlefields were greeted with jeers and cursing. I wanted to honor our veterans and our country, so we held a "Stand Up for America" rally one Sunday morning to give people a chance to show their love for our country.

I invited the United States Army Band to come, and they filled the platform of the church, playing beautiful patriotic music. I also asked the local armory to bring a tank and park it on the lawn. The church was packed, and once again, hundreds of people showed up who had never walked through the doors of a church. I preached on how our nation has been blessed by God and why it's important to show our respect for our land. We had a powerful altar service. We attracted the attention of many new people as well as the press. The next day, the local newspaper ran a front-page article and a picture of our Sunday school kids climbing on the tank. The headline read, "Stand Up for America with Guns of War. Halleluiah!" I didn't mind even that kind of publicity because it attracted curious people to our church.

As our church grew, I had plenty of detractors, mostly other Christian leaders. "Barnett's only interested in numbers," they'd say. "He's just counting people." In a way they were right. I used to say, "We count people because people count to God." I reminded my critics that the Bible included an entire book named Numbers, so numbers must be important to God. I never apologize for trying to reach as many people as possible with the gospel. The Book of Acts tells us that literally thousands were added to the fledgling movement. Then and now, every number represents the eternal soul of a human being. How can we be content to add a couple of new people every year when millions have never invited Jesus into their hearts? We should never be satisfied if our churches don't grow, and growth should always come from leading people to the Lord, not just "sheep stealing" from other churches. The popsicle, the ice cream, and all the other special events were designed to bring new people into our church so they could respond to the gospel. The methods might change over the years, but the goal is always the same: to give everyone who walks in the door of a church an opportunity to trust in Christ.

When people find the Lord, we need to provide ways for them to reach out into the community. The church ought to be the most positive force for good in our cities and towns. That, too, got me into a little trouble. One year, our teenagers stood outside massage parlors and adult bookstores to hand out gospel tracts to the men coming out of these businesses. One of the owners called the police, who promptly arrested our kids and put them in jail. As soon as I heard about it, I was filled with righteous indignation. Most anger is sin, but this kind isn't. It's good and right and holy.

I rushed to the police station and demanded to see the chief of police. When I was finally ushered into his office, I let him have it. "Chief, you're in big trouble!" I began, not too diplomatically. "I already checked with the city attorney, and our kids had a constitutional right to be on the sidewalk passing out tracts. I promise you, tomorrow there'll be a thousand parents and other people from my church demonstrating in front of your police station."

His face went pale. He looked like he had indigestion. He tried to diffuse my anger: "Now pastor, if you'll just settle down and promise not to do that, I'll release these kids right now. Tomorrow, I'll help you get an ordinance to close down these businesses."

He released the kids. I kept my promise not to lead a protest at the police station, but I wasn't finished. The next Sunday I preached a sermon called "We Want Our Rights." I told them I had taken one of my boys to get a haircut, and the magazine rack displayed copies of *Playboy* and other adult magazines. I told them about the time I was picking up groceries and couldn't find my boys because they had wandered off to the magazine section, which was filled with magazines that no one should be looking at, especially young boys. I reminded our people that Christians were the only group in America that didn't demand their rights, but that was about to change. I announced that beginning immediately, we were going to stand up for our rights so we could take our kids to the barber shop or the grocery store and not have to worry about them being influenced by pornography. I asked our people to go to those businesses and very politely tell the managers that we love their business and really wanted to continue shopping there, but if they continued to sell pornography, we'd have to shop somewhere else. We didn't want to, but we would if we had to.

NEWS COVERAGE DURING THE ANTI-SMUT CAMPAIGN

The next day the newspaper headline on the front page read, "Barnett Declares War on Pornography." Only one other group joined us in our effort to clean up our city: the local Catholic churches.

I had no idea what kind of war it would become, but within a few days, we learned that organized crime was behind the massage parlors in our city. The mob bosses tried to stop us. First, I got an anonymous letter threatening to kidnap my kids if I didn't end our boycott, so I made sure I dropped off and picked up our kids from school every day. When this threat didn't work, I got another anonymous letter describing the horrible things they would do to Marja. That got my attention because I sometimes traveled to churches in other cities to teach them about how we had become the fastest-growing church in the nation. But I trusted that God would protect Marja and continued accepting the invitations.

On one of those trips, Marja called me. She was very upset. I asked, "What's wrong, honey?"

She explained that she was driving home from the store when she looked in her rear-view mirror and saw that a pickup truck was following her. When she turned left, it turned left. When she turned right, it turned right. We lived out in the country, and the road was deserted except for her car and the mysterious pickup. Suddenly, the truck pulled beside her and forced her to the side of the road. The driver got out of his truck and started walking toward Marja. Panicking, she jumped out and ran to a nearby farmhouse, threw open the door, ducked inside, and closed the door.

The lady in the farmhouse was frightened. "How did you get in here," she demanded.

"I just opened the door and came in," Marja explained.

The woman's face went ashen. "That's impossible. I just locked the deadbolt and slid the safety chain in place."

I try very hard to look for logical explanations instead of jumping to conclusions of supernatural interventions. Maybe the lady locked her door, or maybe she just thought she did, but I know this: if you're living in the will of God, He'll take care of you.

The man ran back to his truck and drove away. When I got home from my trip, I contacted the sheriff to tell him what had happened. The sheriff told me he knew who the man was, so I asked him to tell me who he was and where he lived.

He responded, "Pastor, you know we can't tell you that. I'd hate for you to do something that might get you in trouble."

I begged and badgered him until he finally broke down and told me that the man lived in a mobile home close to our church. As soon as I hung up the phone, I drove to the address, parked my car, walked up to the front door, and knocked. A woman who I presumed was his wife came to the door. I asked, "Is your husband home?"

She nodded and walked back inside. A few seconds later, a rough-looking guy came to the door. I calmly asked him to step outside and close the door. I told him, "I don't want your wife to hear this." Once the door closed, I looked him straight in the eye and spoke as clearly and calmly as I could. "I know who you are, and I know what you did. What you need to know about me is that I'm not a pacifist. If my wife or kids get so much as a cold, I'm going to blow this trailer up. Do you understand what I'm saying?"

He obviously got the message: "Yes, Reverend, I do."

I turned and walked away, and I never heard from him again. Within a few weeks, the city passed an ordinance to shut down the massage parlors, and the businesses that sold pornography took the magazines out of their stores. But there's more.

The women who worked in the massage parlors were quite upset with me because they lost their jobs. They came to church to see the pastor who shut them down, and remarkably, many accepted Christ and got involved in the life of our church. Earlier, one of our teenagers handed a tract to a man coming out of one of these businesses and told him, "God loves you." The man slugged the kid, knocking him down, but the boy got up and, with blood dripping from his nose, said, "That's okay, God still loves you."

The man went home, but he couldn't sleep that night. He had been raised in church but had fallen away from the Lord. He was so troubled that he came to our Wednesday night service. When I gave the altar call, he came forward and rededicated his life to Jesus.

I'm very proud of the people from our church who stood up for their rights as Christians. Irish statesman and philosopher Edmund Burke said, "The only thing necessary for the triumph of evil is for good men to do nothing." Too many times, Christians complain about all the bad things that are going on in our country, but we seldom do anything about it. I don't apologize for doing a lot of wild and crazy things to get people into church because bigger churches have influence in their communities. Yes, we bused kids in from the barrios and the projects, and when they found Jesus, their parents started attending, and they found Jesus, too. And yes, we reached out to prostitutes and johns, and some of them found new life in Jesus. And yes, we've invited people from every walk of life in every segment of our society to come to hear the gospel of Jesus, and many of them have been transformed by His grace and power. In my opinion, that's how you build a great church. That's how you take back your communities from those who want to destroy it.

We weren't about to stop at popsicles and ice cream.

JOHNNY CASH SUNDAY SCHOOL RALLY AT JOHN O'DONNELL
BASEBALL STADIUM, DAVENPORT, IOWA, 1974

CHAPTER 18

Johnny Cash Comes to Sunday School

*I*n May of 1973, a man named Jimmy Snow invited me to Nashville to hold a revival. I learned later that he was the son of Hank Snow, a famous country and western singer whose career spanned fifty years beginning in the 1930s. Jimmy had found the Lord and was pastoring a church in Nashville. The dates he suggested were clear on my calendar, so I agreed.

I flew to Nashville and began the revival on a Sunday morning, and the Holy Spirit moved in a powerful way. About midway through the week I was sitting on the platform getting ready to preach when Johnny and June Carter Cash came in and sat down in the back. I try not to preach to any one person, but that night I changed my sermon topic to "What Should It Profit a Man if He Should Gain the World but Lose His Soul?" I thought it would be wonderful if people with their influence found Jesus. Many people came forward at the invitation, but Johnny and June remained in their seats.

After the service, however, Johnny wanted to talk with me. "Reverend Barnett, I thought a lot about what you said tonight. I'll be back."

I wondered if he was just trying to be polite and if I would ever see him again, but I learned that later in his own church, when his pastor gave the invitation, he went forward to surrender his life to Christ.

A few months later, Johnny came to Davenport for a concert in the biggest auditorium in town. It was packed, and he put on a great show. I couldn't help but notice how the fans adored him, and I had an idea. After the concert, I went backstage. A security guard stopped me. I asked him, "Would you please tell Mr. Cash that Pastor Barnett would like to talk to him?"

Before the guard could turn to go through the curtain, I heard that unmistakable deep voice: "Let the reverend in."

He seemed genuinely glad to see me, and we had a nice talk for several minutes. He wasn't in a hurry, so I decided to share the idea that had come to me as I watched him perform. "Mr. Cash, I have a dream," I began. "Jerry Falwell just had the biggest Sunday school rally ever. It was so big they held it in a baseball stadium in Lynchburg, Virginia. Why don't we try to beat that and have the world's biggest Sunday school rally in Davenport? Our double-A baseball team plays at John O'Donnell Stadium, and between the field and the stands, I believe we could get 30,000 people to attend. You'll sing, and I'll preach, and we'll call it The World's Greatest Sunday School. Would you consider it?"

He didn't hesitate. "I'll do it, Reverend!"

We agreed on a date, and I went home and started working on it. I reserved the stadium and began advertising that Johnny Cash would be coming to town for the World's Greatest Sunday School. You could feel the excitement build—this was probably the biggest event that had ever taken place in Davenport. Most people were amazed that Johnny Cash would participate. I never talked with him about the particulars, only that he would sing and I would preach. I guess I thought he'd come with his guitar and sing a few songs. People would love it, and I'd then be able to present the gospel to 30,000 music fans. I didn't dream big enough.

The day before the event, Johnny showed up with two semi-trucks loaded with special lighting and a sound system, tour buses with the Carter Singers and Carl Perkins of "Blue Suede Shoes" fame, and his entire "touring caravan" as he called it. What a class act! He held a press conference, explaining he was here because he "believes in Reverend Barnett and what he's doing for the Lord." The newspapers and other media gave it very positive coverage, and the next day, 30,000 people packed into the baseball stadium. I couldn't have been happier. Before we went on stage, however, Johnny threw me a curve ball.

THE RECORD CROWD

"Reverend, would you mind if I opened with a secular song?" he asked. "Some of these fans out there might be a little upset with me if I don't play at least one of the songs they hear on the radio."

"Well of course, Johnny," I exclaimed, maybe a bit too quickly. In those days, especially in conservative churches like ours, no one sang secular music in church. But this was a special event, and I knew it would be a special treat for his fans.

The minute he stepped on stage, the crowd roared to life as he jumped right into "Sunday Morning Coming Down." The lyrics go like this:

Well I woke up Sunday morning
With no way to hold my head that didn't hurt
And the beer I had for breakfast wasn't bad
So I had one more for dessert

Oops! The song was about a man who was hung over from too much partying on a Saturday night, and I suspect a fair number of people in the baseball stadium knew exactly what he was singing about. Of course, those good ol' guys and gals who never spent much time in church loved it, and I didn't receive any complaints from the church-goers, so I guess no harm was done. Johnny and his team put on a fantastic concert, singing a lot of the old hymns and gospel choruses of the church. People were on their feet the whole time, singing along and having a great time in the hot sun. When it came time for me to preach, I spoke about fifteen minutes. Then Johnny and his band played a powerful song of invitation, "Come Home, It's Suppertime," ending with these words:

Come home, come home, it's suppertime
The shadows lengthen fast
Come home, come home, it's suppertime
We're going home at last

JOHNNY CASH AND ME MINISTERING TO PEOPLE WHO ANSWERED THE ALTAR CALL TO ACCEPT CHRIST

As I gave the altar call, over 6,000 people came forward and accepted Christ as their Savior!

As the stadium emptied and Johnny's road crew began tearing down and packing the equipment, it occurred to me that I'd never really talked with Johnny about what to pay him. I knew his normal rate was around $100,000 (probably close to a half-million dollars in today's money), and we had this amount in our budget to pay him—I just needed to check with him on the exact amount so our treasurer could write a check. I caught up with him as he was walking to his tour bus.

I explained, "Johnny, you never told me how much I owe you, and my treasurer would like to take care of that now."

I could barely believe his response. "You don't owe me a penny, Reverend." His craggy face cracked a wry smile as he nodded at me then climbed into his bus.

I later discovered that his $100,000 fee was what he charged when he performed by himself. He had brought his entire team, all their equipment, and extra musicians for our event. Of course, he had to pay them. His expenses included the tour bus, hotel rooms and food, and all kinds of other incidentals, but he was happy to pay it all himself. I believe he felt he was doing it for the Lord, not for me. It was his way of serving the Savior he had recently invited into his heart.

Events like this served a vital purpose: they built the church. I could have remained an evangelist, but I've always felt a great church could win more people to Christ than any individual evangelist, and Westside Assemblies of God in Davenport, Iowa was doing a great job of winning souls for Christ. We experienced an ongoing revival during my time there. In fact, a historic record in the Scott County courthouse documents a "great revival" that came to Davenport, Iowa. It was the greatest revival led by Westside Assemblies of God I've ever seen, but no matter how great the revival, the enemy is always looking for ways to destroy it.

HUNDREDS RESPONDING TO THE ALTAR CALL

CHAPTER 19

Three Movements

*I*t has been my privilege to see the Holy Spirit move powerfully in three remarkable movements that swept through our nation. The first began in the mid-to-late 1940s, and I call it the "healing revival." It was led by powerful preachers like Jack Coe, Gordon Lindsay, and William Branham, and has been described as a "signs and wonders, salvation-deliverance" movement.[2] It drew crowds that numbered into the tens of thousands. In 1951, Jack Coe purchased the largest revival tent in the world, seating 22,000 people. I witnessed miraculous healings as a result of his revivals, and thousands were saved and were filled with the Holy Spirit in meetings across America.

Many of these preachers came to our church and stayed in my parents' home. What I saw was phenomenal: people on crutches

---

2 "The Healing Revival 1947-1958, An Overview," Tony Cauchi, Voice of Healing, September 2011, http://www.voiceofhealing.info/03healingrevival/overview.html

tossed them down and ran for joy, and friends and members of our church who suffered from various disabilities were healed instantly. It was absolutely amazing. This ongoing revival ignited a massive missionary movement that took the gospel across the globe, resulting in exponential church growth that continues to this day. Much of the massive growth of the Pentecostal movement taking place today in Latin America, Africa, and Asia can be traced to this healing revival.[3]

However, I observed that the qualities that made this revival so remarkable were responsible for its demise. People began to expect miracles to take place in every service, and when they didn't happen, false claims were sometimes made. Results were often measured by who had the biggest tent and who took the biggest offerings.

As a result of these excesses, some people began to doubt the authenticity of the movement. Attendance dropped, and fewer churches invited these evangelists to hold revivals in their cities. When I experienced a crisis of faith in my youth, it was a period of doubt about what I witnessed in this movement. Fortunately, my dad wisely counseled me to keep my eyes on Jesus, not on any particular preacher. I believe this could have become the greatest movement of God the world has ever known, but money, false claims, and competition ruined it. By 1960, the once promising revival sputtered to an end.

What can we learn from the collapse of such a remarkable movement of the Holy Spirit? As long as the evangelists kept their focus on winning souls and trusting the Holy Spirit for miracles, they experienced phenomenal success. God used this movement to bring large numbers of people into the kingdom of God. But when they shifted their focus from souls to self, the movement began to decline.

---

3   For more information about the source of this revival in Latin America, read "Why has Pentecostalism grown so dramatically in Latin America?" David Masci, Pew Research Center, November 14, 2014, https://www.pewresearch. org/fact-tank/2014/11/14/why-has-pentecostalism-grown-so-dramatical- ly-in-latin-america/

GREETING ONE OF OUR MANY WHEELCHAIR MEMBERS
WHO RIDE OUR EIGHT WHEELCHAIR BUSES TO CHURCH

It would be easy to criticize these men, but I believe there's a little bit of what took them down in all of us: pride. Instead of recognizing that every good thing comes from God, it's easy to develop a self-absorbed perspective: "Look at me! I'm doing something great for God. We had the biggest revival the city has ever seen," or "Look how much faster our church is growing," or "We just built the biggest auditorium in the city." After a while, God is used as a tool to build the reputations of men. When I give an altar call, I want every lost person to come forward and accept Christ. But whether one or a hundred come forward, the power isn't from Tommy Barnett's preaching but from the Holy Spirit convicting men and women of their need for Jesus. As long as we remember that—and believe it—we'll be fine.

The second sweeping revival during my lifetime has been called the "charismatic renewal," which gave birth to the "Jesus People" movement that reached out to hippies, street people, and surfers. Entire denominations that probably never used terminology like "getting saved" or "filled with the Holy Spirit" were getting saved and filled with the Holy Spirit, including Lutherans, Catholics, and Episcopalians. The movement reportedly began when an Episcopal priest in Van Nuys, California, announced to his congregation that he had received the baptism of the Holy Spirit. It created such a stir that he was forced to resign. He was assigned to a floundering church in Seattle that began to grow rapidly under his teaching about the Holy Spirit.

This movement attracted a wide and diverse following, largely due to its lively style of worship and emphasis on praise. It gave us much of the praise and worship music used today in a variety of traditions, even those that aren't considered charismatic. The charismatic renewal movement also emphasized an informal, come-as-you-are approach to church. It didn't matter if you were black or white, rich or poor, or whether you showed up for church in a suit or jeans and a t-shirt—just come and praise the Lord with us. Consequently, this movement appealed to young people who saw most churches as too formal and legalistic.

One Sunday morning, a young man came to church with long hair and ragged jeans, no shoes, a week-old beard, and his shirt unbuttoned. (I was afraid he might take it off during the service.) The sermon that morning was about loving people in the body of Christ. I said, "We often say, 'Hello. How are you doing?' but instead, we should say, 'Maranatha! The Lord is coming! God be with you!'" After the service as I greeted people at the door, this young man waited patiently to shake my hand. He stepped up, took my hand, looked at me, and said, "What was that greeting you told us about, Pastor? Oh yeah. Marijuana, Pastor. Marijuana!"

I loved the enthusiasm that came with the charismatic movement, and I appreciated their emphasis on praise, but this strength proved to be a weakness. Gradually, Sunday morning services became more about entertainment than teaching the Bible—a time to gather and praise the Lord and feel great that you were a Christian. I'm not suggesting this isn't important, but entertainment isn't the primary goal of the church. Certainly, praise is vital. The Bible commands us to "praise God's holy name" when we gather to worship; to "praise His name with dancing" and "clashing cymbals." When our church offers praise to God, we rattle the rafters. But as the charismatic renewal movement matured, many churches lost their focus on bringing people to faith in Christ. The theme of this revival became "Let's just praise the Lord!" When the church—any church—doesn't place winning the lost at the center of its ministry, it will stagnate and decline.

The third revival movement I've witnessed—and one that continues today—is the "relevant revival." This is a direct response to those who are turned off by church before they even walk through the doors. For a variety of reasons, these people don't feel like they belong in church. They don't see that the church or the message of the Bible makes any difference in their lives. The basis for the relevant revival is clear: "We want you to feel like you belong so that we can lead you to believe." I love that message.

I teach our church that the altar call begins in the parking lot. It's all about making people feeling welcome. Even if they've never been to church, they'll feel at home as soon as they open the door of their cars because friendly people greet them: "Welcome. We're so glad you're here. Is this your first time? Great. Can I walk with you to our Welcome Center?" At the Welcome Center, they're once again greeted with that wonderful word that strangers love to hear: "Welcome!" As they walk into the sanctuary, our ushers aren't there just to help them find a seat. It's yet another genuine "Welcome! I'm so glad you're here today."

By the time people get to their seats, all those fears and prejudices about church have begun to fade. When the music starts, they don't have to feel out of place because the words to the song are projected on screens throughout the auditorium. The worship leader or the pastor begins with another word of welcome and an explanation of what's to come. The goal is for each person, especially those who haven't been before, to feel right at home.

At every step in this process, we're providing a warm, inviting, safe environment. They don't have to wonder where to go . . . we show them. They don't have to know what's happening . . . we tell them. And each time, they have an opportunity to say "yes." When they're greeted on their way into church, they respond. When the music plays, instead awkwardly standing silent, they're singing. When the leader tells a joke or says something funny, they laugh. The whole point of the relevant revival is to make each person feel as comfortable as possible as soon as possible. We even have kids out near the entrance holding up big signs: "Welcome Home!" I remember a guy telling me once that he attended a church for several months before a single person spoke to him or smiled at him. No wonder people don't want to go to church.

By the time the preacher delivers his sermon and offers an invitation to accept Christ, these new friends have been conditioned to respond. It doesn't feel strange or unusual because they're in a welcoming environment and already feel like part of the family. By the way, this might be called a strategy or a method, but it's not insincere. It's not a tool meant to manipulate, but an honest and heartfelt desire of our people to be the most welcoming place in the city. It's like parents who lovingly prepare for their adult children and grandchildren to come home for Christmas. It's not a chore, and it's not phony . . . it's the way we demonstrate love. If you're a soul-winning church, you don't have to encourage your people to be friendly to everyone who walks through your doors. They understand that everyone in the church has a role to play in introducing people to Jesus.

Our model for this approach to ministry is Jesus himself. Jesus said to Peter, Andrew, James, John, and the other disciples, "Follow me." It didn't matter what they had been doing, whether fishing or collecting taxes, Jesus invited them to follow Him in a life-changing journey. He didn't ask for their credentials or if they had the proper training. He just said, "Come. Follow me." From the instant Jesus approached them, He made them feel like they belonged. That's what the relevant revival is all about. "Come on in. You're already one of us."

God has blessed the relevant revival and produced many megachurches across the country and around the world. Our church in Davenport was one of the first to have 4,000 in attendance, but today we see churches that have 10,000, 20,000 and more. I'll be the first to admit that it's difficult to find the right balance between being relevant and not sacrificing your biblical convictions. Over the years I've learned that the best way to manage this balance is to stick to the Bible. Preach the whole gospel. Let people know that your views aren't merely your personal opinions but are shaped by the Word of God. In addition, communicate with humility and grace. When we preach a message on hell, we should have tears in our eyes.

Before you can get people saved, you have to convince them they're lost. The key to being both relevant and faithful is to preach the truth in love, to recognize that we all have sinned and fallen short of the glory of God. Our job isn't to make the lost feel worse, but to assure them that the grace of God is wide enough, long enough, and high enough to take care of their sins. God sent us to heal, not to hurt.

FIRST SUNDAY AT PHOENIX CHURCH, 1979

CHAPTER 20

"Lord, I Don't Want to Go There!"

*I*t would sound poetic and biblical if I said, "It came like a thief in the night," but it happened in the morning. I woke up one day and felt like I had lost the conscious presence of God. I felt like I'd been robbed.

Our church was growing. We'd been in Davenport for eight years. People were getting saved and filled with the Holy Spirit. We were making an impact on our city, and our church's influence was rising. I couldn't accept all the invitations to speak at conferences, conventions, and some of the most successful churches in America. I should have been the happiest, most satisfied preacher in America, but I wasn't. I would rather die than find myself away from God. I was pastoring one of the most dynamic churches in the nation, and I felt far away from God.

I didn't believe God had abandoned me. I was sure of God's promise to always hold me in His strong hands. It was as if I had been walking down a mountain trail with a guide helping me negotiate the path, and suddenly the guide vanished and I was alone. It troubled me deeply.

I tried everything to return to that close, intimate relationship I had known. I prayed and prayed. I went on long walks to seek God. I lay awake at night silently pleading for the presence of the Lord to return, only to wake up the next morning exhausted and feeling more alone than ever. I tried to prepare my sermons, but nothing came. I dusted off old messages and preached them, and people accepted Christ, but I still didn't feel God's presence. It seemed that the more I prayed, the more distant I felt. No one in our church suspected anything because I put on a brave face and acted like everything was all right, which made me feel worse. I stood on the platform as our people sang and worshiped, envious of their enthusiasm and joy, knowing that deep in my heart, I felt alone and forgotten. I longed to feel God's presence again.

One day as I was praying, God spoke to me. When I say that God "speaks to me," I mean that I have a distinct and unmistakable sensation that my thinking is directed to a specific thought. I might be asking God to give me a sermon, and a passage of Scripture will come into my mind or a title pops into my head. I believe that's God speaking to me, and on this particular day, He spoke as clearly as I've ever heard Him.

He reminded me of a letter I had received from a church in Phoenix, Arizona, inviting me to consider becoming their pastor. I remembered it—the letter was from a church that was known as a "preacher-killing" congregation. It had mowed down six pastors in the last ten years. After I read the letter, I said, "Get behind me, Satan" and tossed it in the trash. I was completely content to stay in Davenport the rest of my life, and if I ever considered moving, it would be any place on earth but that church in Phoenix—it's the hottest place in America . . . in fact, only hell is hotter! But the voice persisted: "I want you to call the church and tell them you'll listen to their vision."

Typically, when a church is looking for a new pastor, they invite him to preach so everyone can see him in action, then the board meets and votes to either extend an offer or send him packing. So, to get God off my back, I called the church and agreed to preach at their next Wednesday night service. From the minute I walked into their building in Phoenix, I knew I would never agree to serve there. The sanctuary was dark and empty. It was designed to hold about 1,200 people, but only about 100 were in the room that night—and they looked about as interested in me as I was in them! Instead of all sitting together near the front, they spread out all over the auditorium, adding to the empty feeling and perhaps sending a not-so-subtle message that they didn't like their pastors and they couldn't stand each other. I learned later that this once vibrant church lost most of its members to one of two big churches in Phoenix. That night I would be preaching to the faithful remnant who were barely hanging on.

After the service was over, the church held a business meeting to vote on offering me the position of pastor. The meeting lasted for a little more than an hour. I snuck over to the auditorium where the church business meeting was taking place and put my ear to the door. I know that's not spiritual, but I wanted to know what was taking them so long. As it turned out, they were fighting. I mean they were really going at it! I'd experienced a few squabbles in our church meetings, but I'd never seen anything like this. I began to understand why they had gone through so many pastors.

I tiptoed back to the conference room, and within a few minutes, the board members walked in with all smiles. They told me they had voted me in as pastor—there were three votes against me. Three votes against me! I don't think I had ever had more than a single vote against me, but three? I was devastated.

On the way home, I had a little heart-to-heart with God. "Lord, I don't want to go there. I've got everything going for me in Davenport. It's such an easy church to pastor. The people are terrific. Pastors from all over want to learn from us, and I'm getting invitations to speak around the country."

A thought kept come back: I had always wanted to live in a large city where there are no limits on the people you can reach for Jesus . . . and Phoenix is the fifth largest city in America—no limits there. Could this be the fulfillment of this dream? Maybe, but I needed a little more encouragement.

Once again, the Lord spoke to me. "If you go, I'll give you a hundredfold what you have in Davenport."

I'm not that great at math, but I'm sharp enough to figure that a hundred times 4,000 is 400,000. That got my attention because I've learned that God always keeps His promises. Somehow, He would accomplish great things at this dismal church if I agreed to accept their invitation. Besides, if this was where He wanted me, I had no choice but to obey. But I still wondered how God might fulfill the sweeping vision He had given me.

When I returned to Davenport, I experienced excruciating pain and a blood clot in one of my eyes. I went to see my doctor, and after examining me he said, "You've experienced some kind of emotional trauma, maybe a death in the family or some intense stress." He wrote a prescription, and eventually the pain subsided and my vision returned. I hadn't realized how much of a struggle I experienced over this decision.

The day after I saw the doctor, I told the board I would be leaving. That wonderful church was kind and gracious, agreeing with me that when God opens a door, our only response is to walk through it.

I'll never forget driving away from Davenport with our young family. We had knocked on every door in the city inviting people to church, and thousands of people had found the Lord. Little children from the poorest neighborhoods climbed aboard our forty-seven buses every Sunday and Wednesday and learned about Jesus—and then went home and told their parents about Him. I was leaving a vibrant church of loyal people who love the Lord, and I was now on my way to an uncertain future.

We took two weeks to make the drive to Phoenix, stopping first in Kansas City to see my parents, then on down to Texas to visit with other family members. The Lord used the trip to remind me of my roots: In Kansas City I had been called to preach, and I'd learned to appreciate the rugged beauty of the Texas prairie. I could almost hear God reassuring me, "Everything's going to be just fine. I've got your back."

We left the homestead in Electra, and in a couple of days we passed through Tucson, about an hour from Phoenix. I'd had a lot of time to think, pray, and dream as we drove across the Southwest. My kids never complained about leaving their friends, but I knew they were a little anxious. As we crested a big hill just outside of Phoenix and looked down into the valley at the city, I announced to my family, "We're home! This is where God wants us." My first official Sunday morning worship service in Phoenix was on December 4, 1979.

Shortly after we arrived in Phoenix, the head deacon rented a helicopter to give me a bird's-eye view of the city, especially the suburb of Scottsdale and other areas that were growing rapidly. Then we met the church board in the boardroom in a resort hotel in Scottsdale. I shared all the crazy things we'd done at Davenport—the giant popsicle, the Army tank, the forty-seven buses to pick up Sunday school kids, and all the rest. I thought they would object and ask me to be more conventional, but they wept as they heard how all these ideas brought people to Jesus.

Then I shared my thoughts about church governance: "I want you to know that when it comes to how we spend money, each of you have one vote, just like me. But when it comes to how I operate the church: the programs we add, the guests we have preach, and what I preach from this pulpit, I'll trust God to guide me . . . without your assistance. That's holy ground. Nobody fiddles with my preaching."

After a brief and awkward silence, the head deacon spoke to the rest of the board, "This man needs to run this church the way God wants him to. Let's get out of his way and let him be the leader."

It's funny how a change in attitude can change your perspective. When I walked into the church on my first Sunday, I couldn't believe how wonderful it looked! Dark and foreboding? Not anymore. The church was in a nice section of downtown Phoenix and was built to hold 1,200 people. It was immaculate—everything was bright and clean. A beautiful platform with a choir loft accommodated 150 choir members. They were running around 200 in attendance on Sunday mornings, but I had no idea how many would show up that first Sunday. When a new pastor is announced, people sometimes leave and look for another church. But when the service started, more than 600 people had come to hear the new pastor. The choir chose the opening song, "It's Going to Be a Great Day," and it was. I sat on that platform with my spirit soaring, and I knew this was exactly where God wanted me. I preached my heart out and gave an altar call, and dozens of people came forward to accept Christ. I was thrilled. I thought, *Boy, it doesn't get any better than this!* But it did!

The next Sunday, we had over 800 people, and the following Sunday, 1,000. I had experienced growth at Davenport, but nothing as rapid as this. The fourth week, the building was packed with 1,200 people, and after the service, the board called an emergency meeting. As soon as the meeting was called to order, one of the deacons exclaimed, "We've got to build a new church!" This, after just four Sundays . . . at a place I didn't want to serve.

I asked, "How big a church do you think we need?"

Without hesitation, he answered, "10,000."

I could hardly believe my ears. This was a church that had chased six pastors out of town in ten years and had dwindled to a handful of people. Then I remembered what I had told them in my first meeting with them. When it came to buildings and spending money, I only had one vote. I didn't want to bite off too much too soon. Since I was responsible for filling the place and raising the budget to build it, I countered: "I think maybe we should aim for something a little more realistic, like 3,000."

They decided to table the vote so we could all think and pray about it, and I prayed that they would come to see things my way. A few days later, the head deacon came to my house for lunch. We were sitting at the kitchen table as Marja made sandwiches. We had a little television on the counter, and Pat Robertson (founder of *The 700 Club*) was on, and he was talking prophetically about a coming revival in America. He claimed that very soon the revival would be so great that we wouldn't have enough churches in America to hold the people. Then he looked straight into the camera and uttered these words: "In fact, there's a preacher right now planning to build a new church, and he's going to build it too small."

The deacon punched me in the shoulder, smiled, and said, "That's you!"

We compromised and settled on building a new church that would seat 6,500.

This new chapter in my life began with a season of absence. I had lost the conscious presence of the Lord, but I believe the devastation of abandonment was God's way of getting my attention. For me—and

OUR FIRST CHURCH IN PHOENIX

I'm sure for all believers—the path where God leads us is seldom smooth and straight, but God uses the twists and turns, roadblocks and detours, to deepen our dependence on Him and prepare us for greater things. I hated the feeling that God was so distant, but I loved the result.

GREETING A MAN WHO CAME
TO OUR PHOENIX CHURCH

CHAPTER 21

Changing Clothes, Changing Lives

One Sunday morning shortly after we arrived in Phoenix, I came to church early to pray and prepare my heart for the Sunday services. Suddenly, I heard a loud knock on my office door which opened onto the street. It was very early, and I was the only one in the building, and my first thought was to ignore it, hoping whoever was out there would go away. I didn't expect anybody to meet me there, and I sure didn't want to get mugged before the service! I didn't have a window on the door, so I couldn't look out to see who was there. The knocking got louder, and then I heard a desperate voice screaming, "Let me in!"

Against my better judgment, I cracked the door open. The door was yanked from my hands, and in front of me stood the wildest-looking man I'd ever seen in my life. He was young and had long, greasy hair, a dirty face, ragged clothes, and bloodshot eyes filled with rage. He leaped into my office reeking of urine and sweat.

"Give me money!" he shouted, even though I was only a couple of feet away.

At first I thought he was going to rob me, but his demeanor changed, and he said more softly, "I'm hungry. Give me some money so I can buy some food."

Over the years I'd learned that when street people beg for money to buy food, they're often just trying to get enough money to buy alcohol or drugs. I told him, "I can't give you money, but if you'll come to the church service that's starting soon, after it's over I'll buy you the finest meal you've ever had."

Although I meant every word, I expected him to leave when he found out I wasn't going to give him any money, but he began to cry. He sobbed, "Look at me, sir. I can't go to church like this. I stink. I'm dirty. Look at these clothes."

At that point, I felt ashamed for questioning his motives. I told him, "I've got an idea. If you wait here, I'll go home and get you some better clothes. There's a shower down the hall where you can get cleaned up."

I thought it was time for introductions, so I told him who I was, and he told me, "I'm Scott Wallace. Good to meet you." I handed him a towel and walked out the door to drive across town to our home. As I was about halfway there, it occurred to me that this maybe wasn't the wisest decision I'd ever made. I had just left a desperate man alone in my office. People wouldn't arrive for church for another half-hour or so. He could rob the place or trash my office. What have I done? I ran into my house and got a nice suit, a dress shirt, a tie, and a pair of shoes and rushed back to the church. I had no idea what I'd find.

When I opened the door of my office, he was still there, only instead of those filthy clothes, he was wrapped in a towel. I gave him the clothes, and he went into the restroom to change. When he came out, I helped him slick back his hair and tie his tie. By the time he walked into our auditorium, he looked like a Philadelphia lawyer! As you might guess, I preached to one person that morning. When I gave the altar call, he was one of the first to respond. I'm always thrilled to see people give their lives to Jesus, and rockets went off in my heart when this troubled young man got saved. A few hours earlier, I thought he was going to rob me, but he was now a changed man. I saw it in his eyes. I made good on my promise and took him to one of the finest restaurants in town for a big meal. I learned he had a brother in Phoenix, and the following Sunday, he brought his brother Jack to church.

A Christian for only a week, Scott was already a soul winner. God changed Jack's life, and soon he registered at a Christian college in Dallas. When Jack finished his ministry training course and returned to Phoenix, we asked him to join our staff. He was one of the best hires I've ever made. Jack had remarkable relational skills and loved serving God. He ran our young couples' ministry, which grew phenomenally under his leadership. Then he began leading our Saturday class to teach people to go into their neighborhoods with the gospel message. Jack was a fantastic addition to our staff. Isn't that just like the Lord to turn the frightening experience in my office with a street person into something wonderful?

One day while Jack lifted something heavy in his garage, he aggravated an old football injury. Like most guys, he put off going to the doctor until his wife almost dragged him to the clinic. After a few tests and some x-rays, it was determined that Jack needed surgery. After the operation the surgeon prescribed pain medication to get him through his first few days of recovery. We had never heard of an "opioid crisis" back then, but I had a pretty good idea how to spot a drug addict. Jack got hooked on the painkillers, and when I confronted him about it, he confessed. It broke my heart, but I had to remove him from the staff, and since he was such a prominent leader in our church, I had to let people know what was going on. I stood before the congregation the following Sunday morning and told them that Jack had become addicted to painkillers and would no longer be serving on the church staff.

I thought that was the end of the story, but God still had plans for Jack. After the service, one of our members drove over to Jack's house and offered him a job. He didn't need to lecture Jack about how he had messed up. Jack already knew that. He had been fired, and he needed a job. Thank God for people like that businessman who was willing to take a chance on someone who had failed. But Jack deserves a lot of credit, too. Most people in his situation would have disappeared from the church. They're embarrassed, ashamed, and angry at the church who all too often "shoot their wounded." Or if they choose to go to church, they find one as far away as possible. Not Jack. He never missed a Sunday. He sat near the front and soaked up all the teaching and preaching and joined in the worship with arms raised to the God who hadn't given up on him. I've never seen anything like it. He didn't get bitter; he got better.

Our church didn't shame or embarrass Jack. We were committed to be the place where he felt loved and welcomed, a place where he could heal his hurts and find support. Sometimes I hear people say, "God is a God of second chances," but He's also the God of third, fourth, fifth, and many more chances . . . if we'll turn to Him to accept His love and forgiveness. That's what Jack experienced.

After about a year and a half of faithfully attending church with us, elders of Fairlane Assembly of God, a struggling church in Detroit, Michigan, asked Jack to serve as their lead pastor. He met with them and confessed everything: his addiction, his relapses, and being dismissed from his position on the church staff. He held nothing back. But he also expressed confidence that the Lord had delivered him, and if they could accept him knowing what he'd done, he would be honored to lead the church. I contacted the head elder of the church and assured him that I believed Jack had been truly repentant and how he had continued to be involved in the church. I gave Jack my full recommendation because I had watched him humbly restore his relationship with God and with our church. When the board in Detroit met, it was unanimous. They offered Jack the position, and he accepted.

When Jack arrived in Detroit, he found a church with a couple of hundred people barely hanging on. They met in a small building in a rundown section of town. The budget was so small they could barely pay him and have enough left over to pay the light bill. But to Jack, it represented an opportunity to give back to God. He jumped in with both feet and began knocking on doors, inviting people to church,

PASTOR JACK WALLACE AND ME

getting a bus ministry started to bring kids in for Sunday school, and giving altar calls. He did all the things you need to do to build a great church. Within just a few years, they outgrew their building and bought a beautiful new facility that seated 4,000 people. Soon, they had to expand because they ran out of room again. The church eventually grew to become one of the largest multi-cultural, multi-ethnic congregations in the nation, and it was given a new name: Detroit World Outreach, reflecting its influence around the world. Later, when I was raising money for the Los Angeles Dream Center, Jack's church sent me a check for the biggest amount I'd ever received from a church up to that time: $50,000!

Remember how all this started: That dirty, scraggly young man who demanded money for food came to Christ, then brought his brother to faith, and his brother became one of America's most gifted pastors, who eventually poured into my own ministry. Jack became Bishop Wallace!

Tragically, Jack died instantly of heart failure a few years ago as he stepped off a plane in Brussels, Belgium, where he had gone to speak. He was still young—only forty-seven years old—and he left behind two little girls and a lovely wife. As I attended his memorial service, I couldn't help but think about my dad's philosophy of ministry: go after the ones nobody else wants. When God grabs hold of someone's heart, there's no telling what can happen.

And when He gets hold of a church, watch out!

72 ACRES ON THE SIDE OF THE MOUNTAIN WHERE THE NEW CHURCH WILL BE BUILT, 1982

CHAPTER 22

Growing Pains

*L*eaders are always interested in growth. When I was in Davenport and then in Phoenix, I was invited to speak at churches and conferences all over the United States and overseas to explain how our church was growing. I enjoyed these opportunities, but I also had a church to lead, so I needed to find a different way to communicate with pastors. Instead of traveling to them, we invited them to come to us, and we shared our strategies and how God had blessed us with phenomenal growth.

We called it Pastors & Leaders School (now known as the Dream Conference). The event is filled with practical input about how to build great churches. I shared the things that worked for me in reaching out into the community. I explained that little things matter, like my conviction that the altar call begins in the parking lot before the church service starts, running a bus ministry because if you get kids in church their parents will follow, and encouraging people to follow their dreams for their ministry. But most important, I told the pastors how to get people saved and keep them in church.

Over the years, we've had 250,000 pastors come through our Pastors & Leaders School. In the first chapter, I explained that when

I travel to cities in this country and around the world, God invariably impresses me with the desire to build great churches in them. The Pastors & Leaders School is the primary way He is making this vision a reality. The response of the pastors always surprises me. At every event, we have a wonderful time together. We want to encourage as well as equip. At the risk of reducing the attendance at future Dream Center Conferences, I can let you in on our secret to growth: effective evangelism.

Obviously, there are plenty of nuances to this strategy, but the fact remains that the best way to grow a church is to lead people to Christ and for them to be filled with the Holy Spirit. If a church employs all the wonderful marketing techniques to get people to come to church, and if it has wonderful music and preaching, but people don't trust in Jesus as their Savior, it's only a club. On the other hand, if the new people coming to church trust in Christ, growth will take care of itself. Changed lives are your greatest "advertisement" in your community.

It had happened in Davenport, and it began happening in Phoenix. Someone's husband found the Lord, and his neighbors noticed a difference in him. He was so excited about what had happened to him that he practically dragged his neighbors to church, and they experienced the forgiveness of Jesus. So now you have a half-dozen new "evangelists" letting their lights shine. After a short time, the church in downtown Phoenix that was almost empty before I got there was full of people eager to hear about Christ, respond to Him, and serve Him with all their hearts. We had outgrown our building, and we needed to buy some property and build a new church. Unfortunately, we didn't have any money . . . or at least, not enough to move forward with our building project.

In 1982 we found a seventy-acre parcel of land on the side of a beautiful mountain, but the only way we could buy it was to sell our

THE BEGINNING OF THE PASTORS SCHOOL
PARADE OF MINISTRIES

THE CROWD AT THE PASTORS SCHOOL

church building. We sold it, but we still didn't have enough money. That left us with a dilemma: we had no place to worship and not enough money to build, but we trusted God to come through. The next year we were able to rent Phoenix North High School. Like many inner-city schools, it had recently closed due to a rapidly declining enrollment. Designed to accommodate 2,500 students, the number had dropped to around 800. The school system had no choice but to close the campus and send the remaining students to one of the other city high schools. It was an answer to prayer because the school was only a few blocks from the church we'd been in, and it provided all the space we needed. Remarkably, instead of seeing our numbers decline, as they often do in times of transition, we packed the place, using our tried and true church growth strategy: introducing people to Jesus and His wonderful gift of salvation. After every sermon, I gave an altar call, and people streamed to the front of the high school auditorium to accept Jesus. Marriages were restored, people were freed from addictions and other destructive behaviors, and entire families came to the altar to accept Christ. It was fantastic!

Quite often, when things are going incredibly well for God's people, the enemy goes to work—and things were going really well for us. One evening about a year after we moved into North High School, I got a call from one of our elders.

He asked gravely, "Pastor, did you see the news?"

I could tell by the tone of his voice that the news wasn't good. He continued, "The federal court has ruled to reopen the school. We're going to have to find a new place to meet."

I was stunned. A group was suing the school district, demanding that they reopen the school even if it meant they would lose money. Financially, it made no sense for the cash-strapped school district. The case went all the way to the Supreme Court, which ruled against the school district, and they were forced to reopen the school. We

INSIDE ONE OF OUR 40 BUSES IN THE PHOENIX FLEET, BRINGING CHILDREN TO CHURCH

SIDEWALK SUNDAY SCHOOL BUS

had planned to be in the school until our new church was built, but we had to move—and move quickly. We needed a facility that would hold several thousand people with a parking lot big enough for forty buses. The only one large enough and available was another vacant high school—East High School, but it was eighteen miles away, almost to Scottsdale!

At first, I was devastated because I was afraid we would lose people who didn't want to drive that far. And I was right. We lost some families. I don't really blame them, but in God's providence we gained a lot of new people from the area around East High School, and once again, our church experienced exponential growth.

Finally, our new building was ready, which was wonderful news, but it presented yet another potential problem. Once again, we were moving across town, this time close to twenty miles. Although we did our best to prepare our people for this move, I was worried that by now a lot of families would be annoyed at being uprooted again. Not only that, we were moving into a building that at the time was the second-largest church building in the United States. As the date of our first service approached, I stayed awake at night praying, "God, will anybody show up? Are we going to have the biggest empty church building in the United States?" I was really worried.

Our first Sunday morning in the new building was January, 27, 1985, and I got to the church early that morning. The parking lot was empty, and the vastness of the empty parking lot didn't do much for my confidence. I went into my office and tried to prepare my heart for the service, but all I could imagine was the potential disaster of a tiny crowd rattling around in that big auditorium. Had we made a mistake? Did we build something too big? If people come and see so many empty seats, will they look for another church?

About fifteen minutes before the service, I went to the door to the platform, cracked it open to take a peek, and couldn't believe what I saw. Every seat was filled! People were standing along the walls and at the back of the auditorium. The auditorium was built to seat 6,500, but close to 7,000 people had come. I hoped the building inspector hadn't decided to drop by that morning. I quietly closed the door and struggled with another emotion: fear.

I prayed, "Lord, I'm not capable of preaching to a crowd like this. Please send your Holy Spirit to work through me today."

A few minutes later, I walked onto the platform. I had prepared a sermon about the beauty of the ancient temple in Jerusalem—the cherubim, massive stones, the golden altar, and the stunning beauty of the place of worship, and I was going to compare it to the glory of this lovely new building. But as I walked to my place, the Lord spoke clearly to me: "I don't want you preaching that message. I don't want this building to take away from My glory." The Holy Spirit directed my thoughts to the passage in Song of Solomon: "He is altogether lovely." I believe God was warning me that I might have been placing too much emphasis on what *we* had done as a church and not enough on what *God* had done.

"If this building takes the glory away from God," I began, "let it be destroyed and leveled to the ground. If the great fleet of buses that brought so many here today takes glory away from God, let them be destroyed. And if your pastor brings glory to himself instead of to God, may God cut me down from behind this pulpit and put another man here that will give God the glory."

A lot of people were surprised by my message, but I meant every word. I'm a builder. I loved the whole process of building a large and beautiful church. Sometimes I even feel a bit deflated when we finish a building project. But the Lord got my attention that morning. None of what we had accomplished amounted to anything if it detracted from God's glory. He *is* altogether lovely, and as long as we remember that and keep it front and center in our minds, He will accomplish His will through us . . . beyond our wildest dreams.

The Lord blessed our church that day. At the end of the service, people streamed to the altar seeking more of God and His Spirit. It became a historic moment in the life of our church. God reminded us that God's temple isn't a building; it's every one of us, individually and collectively, and I believe that's why we prospered at this new building from the beginning. God wants to bless us more than we can ever imagine and in ways we don't expect. His plan for us is always greater than ours. We just need to get out of the way and let Him work through us.

AN OVERFLOWING RESPONSE TO THE GOSPEL

WITH LARRY KERYCHUK, FOUNDER OF THE ATHLETES' MINISTRY

CHAPTER 23

Never Dash a Dream

One morning in January of 1980, not long after I had arrived in Phoenix, I was sitting at the kitchen table drinking coffee when the doorbell rang. Thinking it was either somebody trying to sell me something or get me to sign a petition, I grumbled under my breath as I walked to the front door. It turns out, it *was* a guy trying to sell me something: a dream.

When I opened the door, a man introduced himself as Larry Kerychuk. He said, "Pastor, I attend your church. May I come in and talk with you?" I didn't recall seeing him at church, but I'm always glad to get to know our members, so I invited him in and poured him a cup of coffee. We sat down in the living room. We got to know each other, and he told me that he used to be a professional football player for the Edmonton Eskimos in the Canadian Football League. Then he got down to business. He began, "Pastor, I have a dream of our church holding a big conference for athletes from all over the world so we can disciple them. Athletes have a great influence, and I'd like to equip them to be able to share the gospel. I believe God will give me a facility where we can bring the best athletes in the world to train for the Olympics. I'll disciple them while they're here and get them filled with the Holy Spirit."

I listened politely, but to be honest, the dream was so big I didn't think it would ever happen. But I certainly didn't want to discourage him. I smiled and said, "Praise God. What a great vision!" I meant it. He obviously believed this was God's big idea, and he was willing to invest his time and energy. Whether it ever came true or not, I wanted to encourage him.

About two years later, Larry held his first conference at our church, and about 200 athletes came. It wasn't the number he was expecting, but it was a start. The following year, about 600 attended, and I began to think, "Maybe he's onto something." The next year, he had to move the conference to a resort in downtown Phoenix to accommodate 1,200 athletes. Some of the most famous athletes in the country at that time spoke at the event, including Evander Holyfield, Joe Namath, Larry Fitzgerald (Arizona Cardinals), Barry Sanders (Detroit Lions), David Robinson (San Antonio Spurs), Deion Sanders (NFL and MLB star), and more. Legendary Dallas Cowboys coach Tom Landry gave a wonderful message. The purpose of the conferences was to build the faith of these influential athletes and challenge them to share Christ with others, and Larry was getting the job done in an impressive fashion.

But he wasn't finished. His dream was twofold. The first part of his dream was accomplished in those remarkable conferences; the second part involved a facility to train Olympic athletes in a world-class facility that someone was going to *give* him. Larry's dream wasn't too big for God. The owner of Phoenix Track and Swim Club—one of the finest facilities of its kind in the nation—heard about Larry's vision and *gave* it to him! That's right. Larry's specific dream for a facility to train athletes came true.

ATHLETES' SUNDAY

Just as Larry had envisioned, athletes from all over the world came to train. He invited outstanding coaches to bring out the best in each athlete. Every evening, Larry discipled them to build their faith. By the time the Olympics took place in 2000, fifteen of our athletes qualified for the games in Sydney, Australia. When they extinguished the Olympic flame, the athletes who had trained at Larry's facility had won six gold medals, four silvers, and four bronze—if this team were a nation, it would have finished fourteenth in the medal count!

When the early Christians were struggling, the apostle James gave them a pep talk, telling them that they weren't getting what they wanted because they didn't ask God for it (James 4:2). I paraphrase his statement: "If you want to see what God can do, dream big." Larry's dream was huge. When he shared it with me in my living room, I could have asked him to scale it back so it would be more attainable, but I've learned that if God is behind a dream, big things happen. And the only way to find out if God's behind it is to chase it until it either falls apart or is fulfilled. Of course, Larry had to put in long hours and face plenty of discouragement along the way, but the God-inspired dream kept him going, just as it did for Leo Godzich.

Leo was the son of a Polish immigrant who had survived the Holocaust. He came to church one Sunday. He and his wife Molly sat in the third row. At the end of the service, he rushed up to me and announced with supreme confidence, "Someday, Pastor, I'm going to be on your staff."

I smiled but thought to myself, *That's never going to happen.* Leo came back every Sunday, and I could tell he was moved by the messages I preached. One Sunday he approached me with a big idea: "Pastor, how would you like to speak to 3,000 French people?"

I wondered how he had connections with that kind of audience. I didn't know a single French person in all of greater Phoenix. I responded, "Leo, I'd love to."

PASTOR LEO GODZICH,
FOUNDER OF THE MARRIAGE MINISTRY

One Saturday afternoon I was in my office finishing my sermon preparation when the phone rang. It was Leo. He told me, "Pastor, tomorrow's the day!"

He couldn't see me smiling at his obvious excitement. I asked, "What are you talking about, Leo?"

"The French people are going to be in church tomorrow, but I've got to apologize. There won't be 3,000. Only 2,000." He paused for a few seconds to let this news sink in, and then he asked, "Do you mind speaking through an interpreter? I've got one scheduled to be there."

I responded, "Of course not, Leo. I don't mind at all."

The next morning when I parked in my usual place, some greeters rushed up to me looking like they had some kind of emergency. As it turned out, they did. Make that, *I* did.

"Pastor," one of them began. "A large group of people—people we've never seen—are already in the auditorium . . . and all of them speak in tongues!"

I practically ran into the building. I saw Leo, smiling broadly, along with a crowd of men and women. I hoped Leo brought the interpreter! He did; it was his brother who owned a company in France. Every year he rewarded his top 3,000 sales people with a trip to experience America's West. Leo convinced 2,000 of this year's winners to come to our church, and now I would have the opportunity to speak to them. Leo introduced me to his brother, and we went up to the platform together. As I looked at the congregation, I was amazed to see the French men and women singing and raising their arms. When I stood up to preach, I paused after every sentence or two for Leo's brother to translate my message to our guests. When I gave the altar call, 1,600 of the French men and women came forward and accepted Christ as their Savior! When they got back to the hotel, Leo baptized every one of them in the hotel swimming pool!

A few weeks later, we hired Leo Godzich on our staff team. Leo started one of the greatest marriage ministries in America: The National Association of Marriage Enrichment (N.A.M.E).

Things like this don't just happen. They begin when God plants a seed of faith in the hearts of His children. God gives every Christian a job to do, but most of the time we're content to sit back, enjoy the worship and fellowship of a good church, and let someone else do the heavy lifting. Or we wish we could do something great for God, but we don't think we're smart enough, rich enough, or talented enough. Most of the people who launched successful ministries through our church were a lot like Larry and Leo. In many respects, they're very ordinary, but had two things in common: a dream and an unquench-able thirst to obey God. When they heard God tell them what He wanted them to do, they never looked back. Over the years, pastors and other leaders have looked at our ministry and with a puzzled look on their faces said, "Tommy, you seem to have very ordinary people, but they do extraordinary things. How does this happen?" The an-swer is simple: When you find people who have a genuine love for God and a God-sized dream, He "is able to do exceeding abundantly above all that we ask or think, according to the power that works in us" (Ephesians 3:20).

I could share hundreds of stories of seemingly ordinary people who've done extraordinary things for God. Some of those endeavors are global, like the Master's Commission, started by Carmen Balsamo, an Italian immigrant, and led by Lloyd Ziegler after Carmen's untime-ly death. Many other churches have adopted this method of training, and over the years, thousands have been discipled through Master's Commissions and are ministering in countries around the world. Can you imagine the impact we could have on the world if all Christians followed the dream God gave them? Recently I was approached by a pastor who asked, "Tommy, what's your secret?" It's not a secret at all. In fact, it's exactly what Jesus did: inspire ordinary people to do extraordinary things for God.

MASTER'S COMMISSION STUDENTS, FOUNDED AT PHOENIX FIRST IN 1982

AN ELEPHANT USED IN ONE OF OUR
ILLUSTRATED SERMONS

CHAPTER 24

You Can't Fight Love

*D*ecades ago when I was an evangelist, I drove past Angelus Temple, the historic and magnificent church built in Los Angeles in 1928 by Aimee Semple McPherson. I sensed a strong impression from the Lord: "Someday you're going to be the pastor of that church."

At that moment, I thought, *That will never happen!* But the dream was planted in my heart that day. McPherson was the greatest woman evangelist and pastor in history, and the church grew to become the first true megachurch, long before anyone had coined the term. To become the pastor of that famous church seemed like too big of a "What if?"

I forgot about God's promise during my years serving as a pastor in Iowa and Phoenix, but in October of 1991, I received a letter from one of the leaders of the California district of our denomination, Dr. George O. Wood (who later became the General Superintendent of the Assemblies of God). He asked me to move to Los Angeles to pastor Bethel Temple, a small, struggling church which had been the first church launched out of the 1907 Azusa Street Revival in the city. He explained that he wanted to come to Phoenix and discuss the invitation with me. Even though I wasn't interested, I agreed to meet with him. These are excerpts from Dr. Wood's letter:

October 17, 1991

Reverend Tommy Barnett
FIRST ASSEMBLY OF GOD
13613 North Cave Creek Road
Phoenix, AZ 85022

Dear Tommy,

I just wanted to take a moment and send you a follow-up note to that of Ray Rachels' September 23rd letter.

To paraphrase the visionary call to the first missionary church planter (Acts 16:9): "COME OVER TO LOS ANGELES AND HELP US!"

There is probably not a more important city in the world than Los Angeles. A great city needs a great Church. Today, the Church in Los Angeles is weak and powerless. A strong Church in Los Angeles will penetrate all of California, the United States, the Pacific Rim, and the earth with the Gospel.

Research I have done indicates that Los Angeles County is probably the most ethnically diverse of any comparable geographic space in the world.

Within Los Angeles is the largest Mexican population in the world outside of Mexico City. In addition, Hispanic peoples comprise 120,000 Cubans, 100,000 Guatemalans, 200,000 San Salvadorans, 60,000 Peruvians, 45,000 Argentineans, 16,000

Chileans, 10,000 Brazilians, plus a multitude of Spanish-speaking people from yet other countries.

The Asians are also in Los Angeles: the largest Korean population in the world outside of Soul is here, the largest Filipino population outside of Manila, the largest Japanese population outside of Japan. It is estimated that within Los Angeles County there are:

- 170,000 Chinese

- 300,000 Japanese

- 50,000 Cambodians

- 170,000 Vietnamese

- 350,000 Filipinos

- 70,000 Indians (the country)

- 340,000 Koreans

- 30,000 Laotians

- 60,000 Samoans

- 20,000 Tongans

- 100,000 Thais

Within Los Angeles County, there are 1.2 million blacks.

People from the Middle East are here: 300,000 Arab Americans, 400,000 Iranians, 500,000 Jews (many of whom are Israelis), 40,000 Palestinians.

You know that here is the communication center of the world. What a day it would be if Hollywood could be known more for its Christian community than for what it is now! All forms of media are here in Los Angeles: film, print, broadcast, you name it.

Here is the home of the great professional teams which draw world attention: the Los Angeles Dodgers, the California Angels, the Raiders, the Rams, the Lakers, the Kings.

The greatest universities in the world are here: UCLA and USC – and a myriad of private and public colleges and junior colleges. Conversely, the poor and uneducated, the homeless and the outcast are here as well!

Here is the drug and gang capital of the world, the divorce capital, the pornography capital, the abortion capital. You name it – it's here in abundance: including the cults, and the various world religions.

What is not here is the Church!

Within the city of Los Angeles itself, our directory shows 15 churches. Not one of them exceeds 100 people! There are 11 other Assemblies churches in Los Angeles Section: the largest has 400, another about 150, and the remainder less than 100.

Outside of the Assemblies there are only a handful of larger evangelical/Pentecostal churches.

I know it would be terribly difficult for you to leave Phoenix. God has wonderfully blessed you there. It is almost ridiculous for us to even ask you to consider Los Angeles. You pastor one of the world's largest churches – here, you would take one of the smallest. But, we do have this to offer: the greatest mission field in the world!

So, it's a cry from our hearts: "Tommy, come over to Los Angeles and help us!" Not only are we saying that: more importantly, the millions of people without Christ in this area are saying it. They need the help of Christ. A small church will not do in a day of vast challenge. The world's greatest church needs to be in Los Angeles, because the greatest need is also here!

We're praying for you that you will know in the quiet of your own heart what God's will is for you.

Your friend,

George O. Wood
Assistant Superintendent

George and a colleague, Ray Rachels, who was the Superintendent of The Southern California District of the Assemblies of God, came to Phoenix to tour our campus and then came to my office. Immediately, they apologized for wasting my time. "We had no idea what you have here in Phoenix," George exclaimed. "We wouldn't have come if we knew what God was doing in this church."

Our campus is large and beautiful, and the setting is gorgeous on the side of Shadow Mountain. Our lovely prayer chapel is open twenty-four hours a day and is lit at night to invite people to pray. The youth building, which seats 1,200, is fashioned after a Greek amphitheater. The wall opens behind the stage to form a theater in the round, half inside and half outside. Our gymnasium would be the envy of many colleges, and our children's building provides 30,000 square feet of space to minister to our kids. Our auditorium seats 6,000 with two balconies and a platform big enough for elephants, tigers, and Harley Davidsons. All at once.

I could tell George and Ray were a little embarrassed and were wondering why they had come to ask me to pastor a little church in a rough neighborhood where the current pastor was eighty-five years old. But I encouraged George to share his vision because over the years I've learned that if God is behind something, it can't fail.

PHOENIX FIRST ASSEMBLY

George explained, "We need a great church there. I've looked all over the nation, and I've noticed you've always had a heart for the poor, the hurting, and the needy. I believe you could build the greatest church in the world in Los Angeles. I know now that this is crazy, asking you to leave this place, so don't even answer me now. Will you just pray about it?"

As he finished, I remembered the Lord telling me forty years earlier that I would pastor there. But this wasn't the magnificent Angelus Temple—it was Bethel Temple, a struggling little church with a handful of people in their eighties

A lot of people have asked me what you do when the call of God is delayed and looks like it's denied. You do exactly what I did forty years earlier: you listen and acknowledge it, but if it doesn't come to fruition right away, you continue doing your best in your current role. If it's God's will, He'll bring it back to you. I don't believe you can miss the will of God, because if you miss it, He'll bring it back around. As I listened to George and Ray, the memory of the word from God many decades earlier caused me to pay close attention.

They asked me to pray about it, and I did. For five years! During that time, Marja and I occasionally drove to Los Angeles and looked around the neighborhood of this little church. Each time, I got headaches, and I *never* get headaches. On each of these trips, Marja asked, "Tommy, do you think God is calling you here?"

I always answered an emphatic, "No!"

And she always smiled and sighed, "Thank you, Jesus!"

Still, I couldn't get that little church off my heart. Against my better judgment, I contacted George and told him I could pastor at Bethel Temple two days a week—my day off and another day—but I couldn't leave our church in Phoenix.

"Pastor," he answered. "I know it's God's will. I'd rather have you here for a couple of days a week than to close the church. I really believe God wants you there."

With fear in my heart, I approached my board to ask if they would release me for two days each week. Some of them wondered if I could adequately handle both churches. It was a reasonable question. This was before churches had the concept of multiple campuses, so none of us had seen anything like this work. As we wrestled with this question in our board meeting, a physician, Fred Miller, stood and gave a message in tongues, followed by this interpretation: "Do not stop this. Pastor Barnett's dreams become reality. God's got His hand upon this, so do not oppose him. This *is* the will of God."

When I told Marja that I thought the Lord was calling me to Bethel Temple, she responded. "You're too old for something like this!" I was fifty-six. She should have known you never say something like that to a man in his fifties! Her comment sealed the deal, but later I learned from a survey taken by Elmer Towns, the great Baptist church growth specialist, that almost every pastor who had taken a church from a small one to a large one did it while he was in his thirties. I love Elmer, but when I read his report, I thought, *Elmer, you didn't count me in your research!*

My plan was to serve as the overseer of the church in Los Angeles and find an evangelist who would serve as the pastor. I began looking for the right person, but I couldn't find anyone. I interviewed a number of men, and I asked several to visit Los Angeles. They were excited about the possibility of coming . . . until they saw the church and the neighborhood. They often gave me a very spiritual answer: "Pastor, I don't believe the Lord is calling me here."

Craig Smith, one of our leading laypersons, approached me one day and said, "Pastor, you preach a sermon called 'A Miracle in the House.' I believe there's a miracle in your own house that's the answer to your prayers for the church in Los Angeles. It's your son, Matthew!"

Matthew? He was only twenty years old. He was an outstanding youth evangelist, but he had no experience leading a church. Craig wasn't buying the reasons I was resistant. He told me, "Pastor, you've also preached, 'Let no man despise your youth.' Don't you believe that?"

I just hate it when people use my preaching against me.

I finally relented. I asked Matthew to be the new pastor, and he readily agreed. We flew to Los Angeles and rented a small apartment for him. As I got in the rental car and began to drive away, I looked in my rear-view mirror and saw my young, white, blonde, blue-eyed son standing on the sidewalk waving goodbye, and I thought, *I've just set my boy up for failure. There's no way he can succeed. He's too young, and he hasn't been trained in cross-cultural evangelism. I'm leaving him with a handful of people—a handful of old people—in a neighborhood full of street gangs. What have I gotten him into?* I wept as I drove on to the airport.

As soon as I landed in Phoenix, I got a call from Matthew. He was almost out of breath. "Dad, you won't believe what just happened. Just a few minutes ago I heard gunshots and ran to the front of the church. There on the steps was a fourteen-year-old boy who had been shot. Blood poured out of his chest, and Dad, he died in my arms. Killed by a drive-by shooter. Dad, what should I do?"

I had to be honest with him. "Son, I've never been in a situation like that. I don't know what to tell you, but I'll pray that God will show you."

The next day was a Sunday—his first Sunday as pastor—and he told the church what had happened. And then he said, "My dad always says when you don't know what to do, take an offering to care for people who are suffering."

Only a few people were there, but everyone gave what they could, which added up to about $30. The boy's family lived across the street from the church. After the service, Matthew knocked on the door, and the boy's mother came to the door. He began, "Ma'am, I'm the new pastor across the street, and even though I only knew your son for a couple of days, I grew to love him. We took an offering to help you with the funeral."

She began to weep. Through her tears she said, "Please come in, Padre."

The house was filled with gang members. They kept telling her they were sorry, but she slapped them and cursed them for killing her son. Matthew sensed the tension building, and he decided he should leave. As he got to the door, one of the gang members grabbed him by the shoulder and spun him around. He feared for his life, but instead of being the object of violence, the young man asked, "Padre, would you pray for us?"

Everyone in the room joined hands and Matthew began praying boldly, asking God to change the city, change the neighborhood, change these boys. As he prayed, the gang members on both sides of him began to squeeze his hands tighter and tighter. He thought they were going to kill him when he stopped praying, so he prayed for a long time. When he finished, he looked at the young men near him. They raised his hand in a gesture that meant, "You're one of us." Matthew took advantage of this opportunity to explain the way of salvation and led them in the "Sinner's Prayer."

Matthew soon learned that getting people saved was one thing, but building a church in such a tough neighborhood was quite another. A few homeless people attended each Sunday and came forward during the altar call, but they never came back. Many of the original church members either died or quit attending when they saw the kind of people Matthew attracted.

One day as Matthew was walking in the lobby between services, a rough looking guy showed up at the church and put a gun to Matthew's head. He growled, "I've got AIDS, and I'm going to kill you and then myself to make a statement about the way this country ignores people like me. Today this gun isn't loaded, but when I come back tomorrow, it'll be loaded, and we'll both die!"

As soon as the man walked out the door, Matthew called me and asked what he should do. I told him if the man was serious about wanting to kill him, there wasn't much he could do but trust God to protect him. The man returned a few Sundays later and ambushed Matthew as he was greeting people after one of the services, shoving the barrel of the gun against his temple.

"It's loaded this time," he sneered at Matthew. "I'm going to kill you and then myself!"

Matthew calmly responded, "If you pull the trigger, I'm going to go to heaven, and you can't scare me with heaven. But if you pull the trigger on yourself, you're going to hell." The man dropped the gun and began weeping. Matthew prayed with him, and he accepted Christ.

These experiences and the lack of growth in the church discouraged Matthew. One Sunday night he called and shared his frustration. I caught a late flight from Phoenix to Los Angeles and arrived after midnight. The two of us walked through the dangerous neighborhood for hours, block after block, praying that God would do something powerful in the community. We both sensed a breakthrough.

A few weeks later, Matthew called. "Dad, Thanksgiving's coming up, and I want to give all the families in the neighborhood a turkey. Can you get the people in your church to donate 3,000 turkeys and send them here in time for Thanksgiving?"

THOUSANDS OF PEOPLE RECEIVING A MEAL
AND TURKEYS AT THANKSGIVING

I went before my church, explained Matthew's request, and asked them to bring frozen turkeys the next Sunday. They responded generously—we got more than 3,000 turkeys, hired a refrigerated truck, and sent them on their way to Los Angeles. While the truck was on the road, Matthew called me and said, "Dad, we've made a terrible mistake. I just found out that the people in this neighborhood really don't like turkey. They like chicken."

I laughed, "Son, just tell them these are chickens on steroids!"

A few days later, Matthew called back to tell me, "It worked. They loved those turkeys!"

About a week later he called again. "Dad, Christmas is coming, and I want every family in our community to have enough gifts. Do you think your church could send us 10,000 Christmas gifts?"

I guess it helps to have a dad with a large church. I never stopped to wonder where he had learned to ask so boldly for things. I asked my church to donate 10,000 gifts. I love the extravagant generosity of the people in our church. They gave for people in the neighborhoods around Matthew's church, even though they had already provided thousands of gifts for children in our own community. We not only got more than what Matthew needed, but a man in our church donated 5,000 new Huffy bicycles! And he has continued to give the same number for years.

The next time Matthew called, it would change my life forever. "Dad, there's a hospital for sale close to us. With all the drugs, sex trafficking, and homelessness around us, it would make a perfect center to help people get back on their feet. It's fifteen stories high and will need some work, but the price they're asking is cheap." This wasn't a neighborhood hospital: it has 1,400 rooms, and its fifteen stories cover 400,000 square feet!

After he explained the enormity of the project, I gulped and asked, "How cheap, son?"

"Only $16 million."

At that moment, I felt like Redd Foxx. I thought I was going to have a heart attack, and I wanted to shout, "Elizabeth, I'm coming home!"

I didn't have the heart to tell Matthew that I thought this dream might be too big even for his dad. I bought some time: "Let me pray about it, son."

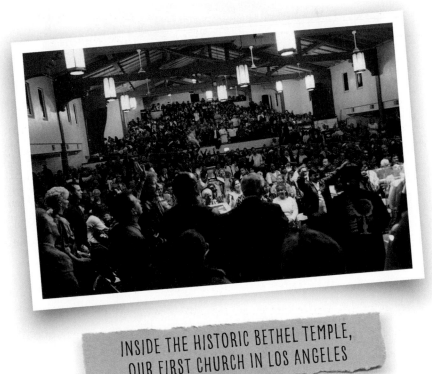

INSIDE THE HISTORIC BETHEL TEMPLE, OUR FIRST CHURCH IN LOS ANGELES

THE LOS ANGELES DREAM CENTER

CHAPTER 25

Provision for the Vision

For many months, I flew to Los Angeles for Matthew's mid-week service to see how he was doing, answer his questions, and encourage him. Sometimes he asked me to preach on a Sunday. About a hundred people trusted Christ every week. I've never seen so much leather and piercings in all my life: earrings, nose rings, and rings in places I didn't want to know about. These weren't your typical buttoned-down Christians, but they were embracing the grace and power of God without the baggage of bad church experiences. it was exciting to see them give their hearts to Jesus, but I learned something about street people: It was relatively easy getting them saved—most of them were desperate . . . at the end of their ropes. But it was hard to keep them and build them into disciples. The pull of the pimps, gangs, and drugs was too strong. Tragically, even though I believe they were sincere about inviting Jesus into their hearts, they often went back to their previous lifestyles.

Over the years, Bethel Temple bought sixteen houses in the neighborhood and rented them for extra income. The current renters were given plenty of notice, and then each house became a refuge for street people who found the Lord. We provided a "father" or "mother" for each house who would look after them and disciple them. Within a short time, all sixteen houses were filled to capacity, but many more people were trusting in Jesus and needed to escape the corrosive influences on the streets.

Not long after I tried to ignore Matthew's idea of buying a hospital, he brought up the idea again. Again, he said it would be a perfect place to minister to the physical, emotional, and spiritual needs of inner-city Los Angeles. Reluctantly, I agreed to go see it with him.

Queen of Angels hospital was owned and operated by the Franciscan Sisters of the Sacred Heart. It was the largest hospital in Los Angeles before it began to decline. The majestic, red-tile roofed hospital occupies nine acres on a hill overlooking the Hollywood Freeway; its fifteen stories have 1,400 rooms. Matthew became increasingly excited as we toured the vacant building, but I wasn't so sure. To me it obviously would require an enormous amount of work and a boatload of money—money we didn't have. I made up my mind that the best way out of it would be to make a ridiculously low offer which, of course, they would refuse, and we would be done with it.

"What do you think?" the realtor asked after we completed our tour.

I answered, "Ma'am, it's really a beautiful building, and it would be a great facility to help us serve the city, but I don't think our budget could handle it." I didn't tell her that our budget was exactly zero.

She smiled, "Why don't you at least make us an offer."

She was playing into my hands, and I was ready to spring the trap. "We're prepared to offer you $3.9 million for the entire property."

Without hesitation, she accepted my offer, and Queen of Angels Hospital instantly became the Dream Center . . . at least in our minds. We still had no money. I had pulled that number out of thin air, fully expecting the realtor to walk away from the deal. However, I wasn't worried. Over the years I've learned that *money follows ministry*. You don't get the money and then do the ministry. You do the ministry, and God sends the funds. If God was in this, He would find a way for us to pay for it. As I like to say, "There's provision for the vision."

Matthew sold his church and the surrounding sixteen houses for $1.4 million. We didn't need them because I asked the sisters to let everyone move in to Queen of Angels Hospital right away with a $500,000 down payment. It was 1994. We started church services on Thursday evenings. Matthew and I invited leading pastors to come and preach. I wanted them to see what we were trusting God to accomplish. I didn't ask them for any money. If they caught the vision, they'd give. Most of them returned to their churches, told their congregations about the Dream Center, took an offering, and sent it to us. Sometimes they invited Matthew or me to come to their churches to share our vision, and they took an offering. Slowly we began paying off the loan, now including interest, a sum of $3.4 million, but we still had a long way to go.

I went on Trinity Broadcasting Network and told our story that Queen of Angels Hospital had officially become the Dream Center. I explained that we didn't know much about cross-cultural ministry, and if anyone in the viewing audience did, please come help us. The next day a man came to us and said, "Pastor, I've been going up and down Hollywood Boulevard every night gathering young people who come here to be movie stars and sooner or later find themselves sleeping in trash dumpsters, abandoned buildings, and under bridges. I take them to my garage and get them saved, but I have no place to get them the help they need. My garage is full and my wife's about to

LOVE KNOWS NO BARRIERS

leave me. Could I bring them to your place?" We let him have a floor of the Dream Center, and he began a phenomenal ministry to these kids. Soon, the first floor was full.

Another man taught us how to help with a ministry he had started. Every Friday night, an army of dedicated young people went out into the streets at midnight armed with a dozen roses. They found young girls—as young as twelve or thirteen—who were being trafficked. They aren't hard to find as they stand on street corners, their little bodies barely covered with provocative miniskirts and tank tops. They're depressed, tired, and used, but they're trapped, with no way to get away from their pimps. This band of brave believers approached the girls, handed them a rose, and said, "You're as beautiful as this rose." Almost always, the girls start to cry and our workers ask them if they'd like to go to a place where they'll be safe, where they'll get help getting their GED and job training, and that it's completely free. Almost invariably, the girls give us the same excuse: "I'd love to, but I can't. See that guy over there? If he sees me going with you, he'll kill both of us."

That's when we go into action. Our people are trained to explain, "Stay right here. In fifteen minutes, we'll drive by in a white van. When we pull up, we'll slide the door open. Jump in and we'll be out of here before he can do anything."

When we pull up to the curb and open the van door, the girl gets in. In seconds, the pimp hops in his car and the race is on. What he doesn't know is that we've got 200 men at the Dream Center in a discipleship program. They haven't been out of prison very long and are barely saved. I love it when those "tough" pimps turn and run as soon as they see our guys standing in front of the Dream Center, their tattoos gleaming in floodlights. Whenever I share the vision for the Dream Center, I repeat Matthew's advice for urban ministry: "Sometimes you gotta go gangster!"

All of the 1,400 rooms in the Dream Center needed to be rehabbed. I went on television again and told people it required $1,500 to rehab a room. If they sent us this amount, we'd put their name on the door. The money started to come in, and we finished one floor at a time.

One day in July of 2000, I got a letter from a pastor in Belfast, Ireland, inviting me to come and preach at a conference. His church had around 200 people in attendance. After thinking and praying, I declined the invitation. He wrote back imploring me to come because he felt it was God's will. I agreed to go.

About two weeks before I was to leave for Belfast, a man called me and asked if I could meet him for tea before I preached at the conference. I never do that. When I travel overseas, I have jet lag and barely have time to get a shower before I preach, so I don't accept invitations for dinners or any other events before I speak. I didn't know this man or anything about him. This time, though, I felt led by the

Holy Spirit to accept. We had a delightful meeting. He explained that he wanted to start a Dream Center in Belfast and asked if Matthew and I would show him how to do it. Of course, I agreed, and then he asked me how the Dream Center was going for us. I love talking about the Dream Center to anyone who'll listen. When I finished, he asked me how much it costs to finish one of the unfinished floors, and I told him: "About a million dollars."

Without missing a beat, he told me, "Pastor, when you get back, you'll have a check for a million dollars waiting for you."

I thanked him, but I'd heard "the check's in the mail" before. When I got home, a check for a million dollars was on my desk! We still had to come up with the remainder of the purchase price for the hospital, and Matthew and I took every opportunity to go out and raise money. With two months to go before we had to pay it off, we were still about $2 million short. If we didn't come up with the money, the bank would foreclose and we'd lose the Dream Center.

A prominent man in our church in Phoenix had been against me going to Los Angeles. His rationale was that my load was too heavy at the Phoenix church to take on another major responsibility in a different city. One day he called and asked if he could go with me to Los Angeles to see the Dream Center. Honestly, I wasn't excited about having him there because I was afraid he was collecting ammunition for his negative point of view, but I invited him to Los Angeles and gave him a tour. He wasn't a very emotional man, but as we walked through the floors and saw girls who had been rescued and drug addicts who had been healed, he was deeply moved. I took him back to his hotel and told him I'd come back in the evening to take him to our church service at the Dream Center. A couple of hours before I was to pick him up, he called and asked me to meet him for a bowl of soup in the hotel restaurant. After we ordered, he said, "Pastor, I've never seen anything like this in my life. I want to help."

A CUP OF WATER ON A HOT DAY

Without knowing what our financial needs were, he handed me a check for a million dollars. He said his son wanted to meet with me, and I had lunch with him the next week. His son was part owner with him in a construction business and had heard what we were doing, and he, too, handed me a check for a million dollars! I hadn't asked for a penny from either of them, and they had no idea that we needed $2 million or we'd lose the building. Maybe that's why we call it the Dream Center!

Crisis averted . . . but we weren't entirely out of the woods. Renovation was only partially complete, so we began tackling one floor at a time. We painted every room, fixed the plumbing, put in new furniture, and when we ran out of money, we stopped until we raised more. We had finished nine floors when the city building inspector came and told us our progress was too slow. He grumbled, "If you don't finish in six months, we're going to have to condemn the building and close you down."

We were heartbroken. We'd put so much work into the building, and the Lord had miraculously provided the funds we needed to complete the purchase. We needed $10.5 million to finish the six floors, but we had no money. I was desperate and reached out to a wealthy Christian company who had given us $500,000 earlier, hoping they might be able to help us. The owner came with his accountant and toured the Dream Center. They pored over our financial records. He appeared to love the place, yet he refused to help us. When I asked him why, he explained that even if he gave us the money to have the building finished, our income wouldn't cover the operational cost of the new floors, and that could destroy us. It hurt, but he was right.

After all that work, it looked like we were going to lose the Dream Center, but one of our finance guys found a computer program that to this day I don't fully understand. It involved a government-approved program where we would partner with banks that would sell tax credits, and we would get a percentage of what they sold. When all was said

A NEW ROOM FOR A NEW START

and done, they had sold $49 million of tax credits. Our percentage? Exactly $10.5 million! Thank God for brilliant and creative people!

Brilliant accounting was helpful, but it wasn't enough to meet the financial demands of the renovation. Some dear friends stepped into the gap for us. Let me tell you about a few of them. When Hurricane Katrina devastated New Orleans in 2005, Matthew wanted to go there to bring 300 families to the Dream Center in Los Angeles. He contacted a bus company to ask about the cost of transportation, and they said they could bring one bus of 60 people, maybe twelve to fifteen families, for $10,000. It was obvious we couldn't afford this price because we'd need a lot of buses. At that time, a man who is a member of Kabbalah, a Jewish sect, came to the church office. He said, "I heard about your need. I'm going to charter planes to bring those 300 families to Los Angeles." As the planes flew into LA, news outlets brought reporters and camera crews, and The Salvation Army and the Red Cross set up stations to distribute necessities to people who had lost everything in the storm. We became the darlings of Los Angeles. Morris Cerullo, a world-renowned evangelist, saw the reports. He drove up from San Diego, and I gave him a tour of the Dream Center and took him to see how we were caring for the people from New Orleans. At the time, the Dream Center was only partially completed, and he could tell we didn't have enough room for all of the refugees. He asked, "What would it take to finish the renovation of one of the floors?"

I told him, "About a million dollars."

Without missing a beat, he responded, "I'll do it." He gave more than a million dollars to finish a floor, and since then has given even more to the Dream Center.

Jentezen Franklin became the pastor of Free Chapel in Gainesville, Georgia, in 1989. It was a church of about 300 people. He attended our Pastors & Leaders School, applied the principles we taught, and his church took off. On one of his Dream Center visits, he discovered that when children exit foster care when they're eighteen, they often end up on the streets. By that time, Jentezen had a very successful television program, and he told me, "I want to bring this need to the television audience and see what God will do." When he went back to Georgia, he shared the need on his program, and a few weeks later, he sent us a check for $100,000. A couple of months after that, he sent another check for $100,000, and then another and another. His ministry has given over $1 million dollars to meet the desperate need of young people who leave foster care. When he learned about all the veterans, men and women, who were living on the streets, he asked if he could provide funds to help them, too. To date, his ministry has given over $1.5 million dollars to the Dream Center.

In 1993, Mike Rogers came from Artesia, New Mexico, to our Pastors & Leaders School. On the last night, I always share the story of the Dream Center and ask people to go up on the mountain behind the church to pray about what God might want them to give. Mike didn't have much money. In fact, he didn't have enough money for a hotel room, so he stayed with some people from the Master's Commission. When he prayed, the Lord put $200 on his heart. He looked in his wallet, and found exactly that amount of money. He prayed, "Lord, $200 is all I've got." He sensed the Lord reply, "That's all I want."

Mike came back the next year, and again, I asked people to climb the mountain and pray about what God would have them give to the Dream Center. The Lord put $100 a month on his heart. He couldn't imagine giving all $1200 at once, but he could believe God for $100 a month over his tithe.

The next year Mike came again and the two of them, Mike and God, had the same conversation, but this time the number was $400 a month. The next year it was $1,000 a month. By this time, Mike's

NO ONE IS LEFT OUT

business was thriving, and he realized he could pray about giving at times other than on the mountain after the last talk in Phoenix. Mike prayed about the amount God wanted him to give before he arrived for the Pastors School, and he pledged $4000 a month. The following year, it was $10,000 a month. The next year, God impressed Mike to give $200,000. He did the math and realized this came to $16,666.66 a month. He told me about his conversation with God: "I told God I had been a Baptist, and that was just too many sixes for me. He told me it didn't bother Him, but if I wanted to round up, that was fine with Him. So I gave $17,000 a month that year." But it didn't stop there. Eventually, Mike gave $150,000 a month to the Dream Center, beyond his tithe to his local church. Since the first night when Mike responded to God's prompting to give all he had, God has blessed him to be able to give several million dollars to the Dream Center, and he has raised much more than that. If you look at his lifestyle, you'd never believe this story. He's a humble man who lives a simple life, but

PRAYER ON THE SIDEWALK

he has the biggest and most generous heart I've ever seen. We named one of the buildings in his honor.

Michael Hammer is the only grandson of Dr. Armand Hammer, the founder of Occidental Petroleum. When Michael and his family visited the Dream Center, their hearts were moved to contribute to what we're doing for God's kingdom. One of the ways Matthew has raised funds is to have people contribute an amount of money for each free throw he makes in twenty-four hours. Michael came to watch when Matthew was almost at the end . . . of his time and his energy. He could barely hold his arms up. Michael told him, "I'll give you $25 for each basket you make." Suddenly, Matthew felt energized. Michael upped his offer to $50 and then $100. Matthew made over 14,000 baskets. By the end of the day, Michael gave over a million dollars. Since then, he has given several times that amount of money to the Dream Center—and he says he's not done yet!

When we renovated the Dream Center, we faced the monumental task of furnishing 1,400 rooms. As always, we asked God to provide. Tim and Resa Hunt have a company building furniture in Spokane, Washington, and they graciously offered to provide everything we needed for all those rooms.

Jack Carey is a businessman in Phoenix who visited our church one Wednesday night with Sandra, his wife. At the time, we were in the early stages of building our church on the side of Shadow Mountain. I was told to look for him. As the service concluded, I asked people to kneel at their seats for a moment of prayer. I walked down from the platform to where he was kneeling, and I put my hand on his shoulder. I said, "I'm so glad you're here tonight. Let me ask you a question: Do you know Christ? Do you need Him?"

Instantly, he replied, "Yes, I need Him." I led him in a prayer and he accepted Christ as his Savior.

A few weeks later, Jack came with me on a tour of the building site, and I shared the vision for what the church could mean to the city. His heart was touched, and he gave generously to our ministry. A few years later, when we launched the church at Bethel Temple in Los Angeles, Jack moved to San Diego. Jokingly, I told him he was leaving Jerusalem for Jericho, and he'd better watch out for thieves and brigands! As Queen of Angels Hospital became the Dream Center, Jack wanted to be part of it all. I guess he meant it: God has used this man beyond anything I could have imagined.

These are stories of amazing generosity, but countless others have given just as generously out of the means God has entrusted to them. Each person has caught the vision to find a need and fill it, find a hurt and heal it, and they see the tangible fruit of transformed lives when they see reports of what God is doing at the Dream Center. No contribution is too small; every contribution is an integral part of changing the trajectory of men and women, boys and girls, who have found renewed faith, hope, and love. I learned an important principle early in my ministry: money follows ministry. In other words, if we step out in faith to reach and care for people, we can be sure God will supply all the resources we need.

Today, every floor is finished, and we're rehabbing all the other buildings on the campus. Our mission is simple—it's exactly what has driven me throughout my ministry: find a way to serve the people who nobody else wants. We're the go-to center for many of the law enforcement agencies and the court system who give those they pick up a choice: jail or the Dream Center. We continue to rescue girls being trafficked, and our alcohol and drug rehabilitation program has one of the best success rates in the region. We're also one of the only places in Los Angeles that will take entire families who are homeless. We distribute a half-million pounds of food to thirty-four neighborhood locations and feed more than 40,000 people every month. We're prepared to meet any physical, emotional, or spiritual need represented by the poor and homeless of Los Angeles. And if a new need comes up, we'll find a way to meet it so we can fill our mission: find a need and meet it, find a hurt and heal it.

With help of the Holy Spirit and a lot of dedicated staff and volunteers, we change lives. I love sharing their stories, but there's nothing like hearing them firsthand. I encourage you watch and listen to them here: https://dreamcenter.org/changed-lives/. I promise, it'll touch your heart. To learn more about how to start a Dream Center in your community, look at the appendix in the back of this book.

Since we opened up the Dream Center, almost 300 other Dream Centers have opened all over the world. We're thrilled that so many people are responding to the needs of their communities and cities in the name of Jesus.

Years after we bought the little church in Los Angeles and started the Dream Center, Matthew told me about a vision he had when he was sixteen years old. He was looking up to the heavens one night and felt God speaking to him: "When you're twenty years old, you'll be pastoring a church in Los Angeles." As I drove away on his first day in Los Angeles, I thought I was setting him up for failure, but God had given him a vision of a remarkable future.

CONNECTING HEARTS

JIM BAKKER SPEAKING AT
THE LOS ANGELES DREAM CENTER

CHAPTER 26

Old Friend, New Calling

I was reading my Bible one day and came to a familiar passage in Matthew where the Lord said, "For I was hungry and you gave me something to eat, I was thirsty and you gave me something to drink, I was a stranger and you invited me in, I needed clothes and you clothed me, I was sick and you looked after me." As I read, I was feeling pretty good about myself. I responded, "I've done all these, Lord!" And then I continued reading. "I was in prison and you came to visit me" (Matthew 25:35–36 NIV). I don't know how many times I'd read that passage in my life, but this time it hit me like a ton of bricks. I was falling short of God's calling in one of these areas.

Despite the fact that our church had one of the largest prison ministries in the nation, and the Dream Center has helped rehabilitate thousands of former prisoners, I had visited very few people in prison. Later in the passage, the Lord said, "Truly I tell you, whatever you did for one of the least of these brothers and sisters of mine, you did for me" (Matthew 25:40). I was missing opportunities to serve the Son of God because I wasn't reaching out to people in prison.

My mind immediately went to a man I had known and loved over the years, but who had recently been sent to prison: Jim Bakker. For over a decade in the 70s and 80s, Jim and his wife Tammy Faye hosted a popular television program, *The PTL Club*, and built Heritage USA, a Christian theme park near Charlotte, North Carolina. After a sixteen-month investigation, he was indicted in 1988 on twenty-four counts of fraud and conspiracy. In fact, as I was returning from appearing on his television program, the news broke. I was heartbroken over the next several days as the extent of his crimes became known. I knew Jim Bakker—he was a good man who had made some very bad decisions. A year later, after a five-week trial, the jury found him guilty on all counts and sentenced him to forty-five years (later reduced to eight). Jim began his term in prison.

I knew what the Lord wanted me to do, but I didn't want to do it. Even though he was a friend, Jim's conviction invited ridicule from many corners of our society, especially condemnation of Christian leaders for hypocrisy. I couldn't visit him secretly . . . the word would get out. I told the Lord, "If I go to see him, my reputation will be damaged."

The Lord responded, "Tommy, your reputation isn't all that hot anyway. Go."

When I arrived at the prison just outside Minneapolis in February of 1993 and was ushered into the visitor's room, the frail-looking former head of one of the largest television ministries and theme parks literally ran into my arms. Jim sobbed, "Pastor, only one other minister has visited me here, and that was Billy Graham." (That made me feel a lot better about my visit! At least I was in good company.) I spent the day trying to encourage him. He was wracked with guilt and shame for what he had done.

A friend once heard me talking about a fallen preacher, and he remarked, "Whenever you talk to leaders who have done something horrendous, you don't have the same attitude of disgust or contempt many others in the church have for them. In fact, you don't even seem to be shocked at all." I'd never thought about that, but he's right. To me, sin is sin. We're all human. People fail, but they don't need to be defined by their failure. Jim Bakker did indeed fail, but it's not my job to pile on and remind him of his mistakes. Most people are well aware of their sin and its consequences for them, their families, and those who trusted them. At that point, they need help to go from failure to victory, and that only comes through God. My message to Jim and others who have fallen is clear: "If you fall, get up. Receive the forgiveness that God loves to offer you. Then go and sin no more."

As the winter sun cast long shadows across the visitor's room, a guard came and politely explained that it was time for me to leave. Jim and I got up, hugged, and said our goodbyes.

After Jim served about five years in prison, he was released. He moved into a farmhouse in rural North Carolina provided by Billy Graham. Jim learned about the ways God was changing the lives of young people through the Master's Commission, and he encouraged his son Jay to enroll. As we planned the next Pastors & Leaders School, we asked dozens of people to give their testimonies. One of those we asked was Jim's son.

Jim heard wonderful reports about Jay and called me. "Pastor, I've learned that my son is going to be giving his testimony at the next Pastors School. I know it would cause a huge problem for you if I showed up, but could I sit in the overflow room at your church and watch my son's testimony on a screen?"

I didn't say anything, so Jim broke the silence: "No, I can't ask you to let me do that. Someone from your church would know, and that would create problems for you. You've done enough for me already.

But what if, after the service starts, I sneak in and sit in the back row? I'll leave before the end of the service."

Again, I just listened and didn't respond.

Jim took my hesitation as a "no." He then told me, "No, Pastor, even that would put you at risk. Would you record it and send it to me?"

Something came over me at that moment and I thought, *A man has a right to hear his son give his testimony!* I told him, "Jim, I'm sending you a plane ticket, and I'll pick you up at the airport."

I met him at the gate, and as we walked through the airport, I felt that every eye was on this once-famous man who had fallen from people's grace, but not God's. I dropped him off at the home of one of our leading laymen and then went to the church to prepare for the service. I felt unsettled. What was going to happen when all these pastors who came for inspiration learned that I allowed Jim Bakker to attend? How will the media respond? (Jim's presence was certain to make the news.) He had only been out of prison a few weeks. He hadn't attended a church service because he didn't feel welcome. I reminded myself that the only thing that mattered is that God would be glorified. If that meant I'd have to take some heat, so be it.

As the evening service began, I was still a little nervous. We began with a parade of our ministries, which is always a highlight of the Pastors & Leaders School. Seven thousand pastors were on their feet clapping and cheering as more than 200 ministry groups marched across the stage to the rousing music from our orchestra. The last group literally skated across the stage: our skateboard ministry. After an extended ovation, I motioned for everyone to sit down. I asked a number of people to give their testimonies, and then Jay stepped up to the microphone.

He began to tell how God had changed his life, and to make sure people understood who he was, he told them, "My dad went to prison because of his deeds. His name is Jim Bakker."

For about five seconds, the place was dead silent. I thought, *Oh no. This isn't going so well!* Then the place erupted in a great ovation. When they became quiet, Jay gave a moving testimony about his faith in Christ.

When he finished, I moved close to him and put my arm around his shoulders. I told him in front of the audience, "Your dad called me the other day. He knew you would be giving your testimony tonight. He wanted to be here, but he offered to stay away because he thought it would hurt my reputation. I told him he had every right to hear his son's testimony. Your daddy's here." I turned to the crowd and said, "Jim Bakker, stand up!"

I held my breath. How would these pastors who had taken heat over Jim's mistakes respond? Once again, the placed roared with deafening cheers and clapping and praises to God as Jim Bakker ran down the aisle and hugged Jay at the front of the church. It was like the Prodigal Son—but this time, it was a father coming back home. They hugged and cried in an emotional reunion. The enormous roar went on for at least five minutes, and there wasn't a dry eye in the audience. When it ended, a voice from the crowd called out, "We love you, Jim!" And another, "We love you, Jay!" I asked Jim if he wanted to say anything.

Jim stepped to the microphone and turned to Jay, "I'm so proud of you." Then he spoke to the audience: "I had to go to prison to get my son back. I flew on Air Force One with the president. I owned the second-largest theme park in the world, and I had a leading Christian television show. But I lost it all, and with it, I lost my son's respect. Pastors, don't win the world and lose your children."

I invited pastors who had problems at home to come to the altar for prayer, and there wasn't enough room. Guys were kneeling around the altar and back up the aisles, and for an hour we experienced a magnificent outpouring of the Holy Spirit. A wonderful prayer meeting broke out as people fell on their faces. Some stayed and prayed all night. Many pastors who were there said it was the most powerful service they had experienced in their lives. It certainly was the most moving one I'd ever seen.

This was certainly a "mountaintop experience," but soon, I was back down in the valley dealing with day-to-day challenges. I discovered that the valley is where we find the most fertile soil for growth.

A GREAT DAY FOR JIM AND JAY

JIM BAKKER AND HIS FAMILY

CHAPTER 27

The Restoration of Jim Bakker

A few months after Jim and his son were reunited at our church, I invited Jim to speak at the Dream Center. He shared his testimony at one of our services, including his downfall and his time in prison. He asked people to raise their hands if they'd ever been in jail or prison, and almost everyone's hand went up. Jim could identify with them, and they could identify with him.

After he spoke, we spent some time together. He told me, "Pastor, I'm struggling. No matter where I go, no one wants anything to do with me. I'm so discouraged. Some days I don't think I can keep going. Would it be okay if I stay at the Dream Center? I feel loved and accepted here, and I need to be healed, too."

Instantly, the same fear about negative publicity clouded my thoughts. Then the Lord again spoke to me, reminding me why we started the Dream Center in the first place. Men and women who had been convicted of murder were living there, and we routinely served people with AIDS, prostitutes, drug addicts, alcoholics, and the homeless. Jim was no better or worse than any of them. Since I truly love Jim Bakker and never want to miss out on God's blessing, I told him, "Of course, Jim. You're always welcome here. We've got a little house on the Dream Center property. It's your home for as long as you need it."

I held a staff meeting and explained that Jim was coming to live at the Dream Center. I wondered if any of them might not want him around, but these wonderful people are all about helping people who are down—and Jim Bakker was really down. I didn't realize how far until he showed up.

Always an impeccable dresser, Jim showed up in a faded pair of jeans and a wrinkled shirt that had seen better days. He wouldn't look anyone directly in the eye and hardly said a word as I took him to the little house that was his new home. It had once been the nuns' quarters. Once inside, he looked around, showing no emotion. I couldn't believe he was the same man who had come to our church in a pair of crisp khakis and blue blazer to hear his son's testimony, but by this time, the reality of his situation had hit him. It wasn't just that he went from living in mansions and jetting all over the world to living in a place that catered to society's untouchables. He had no visible friends, no money, and no hope. He once had people crowding around him, wanting to appear on his show, but now people avoided him.

Jim settled into the house, and a few days later I got a call from Armondo, one of the Dream Center staffers. "Tommy, none of us have seen Mr. Bakker since he got here, and we're a little worried. What should we do?"

Had it been too much for him to come to a facility like ours? Had he slipped out one night? It happens. I told Armondo to let himself into the house to check on Jim. He found Jim had barricaded himself in his room and away from reality. It was clear to all of us that Jim was suffering from depression. Our people had seen this before—it's quite common when people hit bottom, and it's not uncommon for people who have made tragic mistakes to isolate themselves.

We developed a plan: Armondo went to Jim's house every morning, got him up, took him for a walk, and then accompanied him to the dining room for breakfast. Some days he took Jim to a movie or to a restaurant for a nice meal. Jim sometimes resisted. He wanted to stay inside and hide from the world, but our wonderful worker wouldn't let him. If Jim locked the door, our man found a key, unlocked the door, and helped Jim face another day.

After two or three months, Jim began to respond. He had lost everything when he was convicted of financial crimes, but he received a small amount every month for living expenses from friends who wanted to help. The first sign that he was getting better came when he walked to a nearby hardware store, bought some paint, and began painting some of the unfinished rooms at the Dream Center. He joined our "adopt-a-block" program that literally transforms the poverty-stricken neighborhoods in the city. On another occasion, he rented a portable Ferris wheel. He had it delivered to our parking lot and asked our workers to spread the word that any child in the community could ride for free. Hundreds of kids showed up, giggling and screaming as they rode it. Jim stood and watched, tears streaming down his face. He was learning something that he probably already knew intuitively: if you're feeling down and need a lift, help someone. Serving helped Jim feel useful. I met with Jim every week while he was at the Dream Center, and I could see that he was getting stronger both emotionally and spiritually.

During this time, I was asked to provide the same oversight for a couple of other fallen prominent leaders, but sadly, neither was willing to humbly submit to the process of restoration like Jim did. Both of these men believed that a quick confession was enough and they could immediately return to ministry, but Jim was patient and submitted to the necessary process.

I suspected that Jim wanted to go back into Christian television, but I cautioned him against it. I felt he needed to spend more time helping others, especially the poor. This, to me, is absolutely necessary to restore fallen leaders. Are they humble enough to work alongside the poor, the forgotten, the unlovely? Are they serious about serving God without any recognition, or do they long to get back into the limelight? Jim had always had a heart for the hurting and disenfranchised. I challenged him to start a Dream Center. He started one in Panama City, Florida, that continues to this day.

While Jim was at our Dream Center in Los Angeles, Marja brought a young lady from our church in Phoenix to give her testimony. Lori Graham had been miraculously saved from the hazards of life on the streets. She had completed our Master's Commission and was serving in several ministries. Marja introduced Jim to Lori. Soon they fell in love and were married. As part of Lori's commitment at the Master's Commission, she drove a bus route sponsored by our church. On the route, she met a mother who was addicted to crack. That's not unusual, but she had two little girls—crack babies—and she couldn't care for them. She realized they would be better off with someone else.

Lori was that "someone else." She grew attached to the two little girls and approached her new husband with a crazy idea: "Jim, let's adopt these babies."

By this time, Jim was in his sixties, the age when most men are enjoying their grandchildren and slowing down a little. No one would have blamed him if he had told Lori he didn't think he was up for the challenge. It meant he would become the father of two girls under three years old—girls who might have neurological problems because of their mother's crack addiction. But when Jim spent time with the girls, he loved them just like Lori did. In the blink of an eye, Jim and Lori became new parents. (This reminds me of Abraham who had a child when he was 100 years old!)

Lori met another woman on her bus route, an older woman who was taking care of her granddaughters because her daughter was in prison. Lori's heart was broken as she saw the two little girls running around in nothing but dirty diapers. Their grandmother was doing her best, but she was overwhelmed by the responsibility. She lived on a small financial allotment from government assistance, but she didn't have enough money for diapers, baby food, doctor visits, and other expenses. Her daughter would be in prison for several more years, and the girls would be grown up by the time their mom got out of prison. Jim and Lori went to the prison to talk to their mother, and she agreed to give up her parental rights so Jim and Lori could adopt them. Not too many couples have four kids before they've been married for a year. Eventually, Jim and Lori adopted a total of nine children, and they have provided temporary care for dozens more in their loving home.

Today, the first two of those babies are young adults who are doing marvelously well. They've gone to college, and they help Jim and Lori in their ministry on *The Jim Bakker Show*. They are lovely young adults who might have never made it out of poverty if it weren't for Jim and Lori's big hearts.

When I watch Jim's new television show and see those kids, I think back on my decision to visit Jim in prison. I was worried about what others might think about me reaching out to him, and I almost missed an opportunity to be part of something beautiful.

My fears weren't justified. I didn't get a single criticism from anyone about helping Jim. Not one. In fact, pastors from all over the country called or wrote to commend me for helping him. I'm so proud of Jim and Lori Bakker. They are amazing people and dear friends.

There's one more part of this amazing story: our staff member, Armondo, who had been initiated into a gang when he was only seven years old. He would probably be dead today, another victim of gang violence, if he hadn't come to the Dream Center where he turned his life over to the Lord. Armondo—or Mondo, as Jim and Lori affectionately call him—never left Jim's side at the Dream Center, and today he serves as the producer for Jim's television ministry.

LA-98— Angelus Temple, Los Angeles, California

AIMEE SEMPLE McPHERSON

PASTOR

OB-H386

Church of the Four Square Gospel

ANGELUS TEMPLE, CIRCA 1930'S

CHAPTER 28

The Forty-Year-Old Promise

I was beginning to wonder what had happened to God's assurance that one day I would be the pastor of Angelus Temple in Los Angeles. When I drove by it forty years earlier, I sensed God's clear promise. The church was founded by Pentecostal evangelist and media celebrity Aimee Semple McPherson. When she found a lot for sale next to Echo Park, she declared, "This is the place God would have us build." She had just enough money to buy the property and hire a contractor to dig a hole for the foundation. When her friends asked her how she was going to find the money to finish the church, she answered, "God told me to dig the hole. Now it's up to Him to fill it."

It was a grand structure, designed by the architect of the Pasadena Playhouse and Grauman's Metropolitan Theater (now Paramount

Theater). The church, completed in 1923, was distinguished by its 125-foot dome topped with a lighted cross that can be seen for miles.

It seems the structure was a bit too grand for some denominational leaders. An article appeared in *The Pentecostal Evangel* magazine criticizing her and her church for taking money away from missions to construct large buildings. That year, McPherson's church had given more money to missions than ever before. She was so offended by the criticism that she pulled her church out of the Assemblies of God and started The International Church of the Foursquare Gospel, today with a worldwide membership of over eight million.

I was convinced God had told me this was the church I would someday lead, but so far, nothing had happened. In fact, it didn't seem likely that it ever would. But I was close: the Angelus Temple and the Dream Center were only four blocks apart.

ANGELUS TEMPLE NEXT TO ECHO PARK
AND DOWNTOWN LOS ANGELES

When we sold Bethel Temple, we began holding our church services in a small auditorium in the Dream Center. Matthew was the lead pastor, and I continued to assist him. As God blessed us with more people, we had to move into the gymnasium, but eventually, we couldn't fit everyone in there. Imagine 700 people packed into a windowless gym on a hot Sunday morning. It didn't have air-conditioning, and we had only a makeshift stage and folding chairs. We had to do something, but I didn't know what.

One day I read in the newspaper that the Angelus Temple had fallen on hard times. Younger members wanted to make major renovations to the building, but older people opposed the changes. When they couldn't come to an agreement, the younger group—the majority—left and started a new church in Pasadena. Decades earlier, during Aimee's day, the church's 5,300 capacity auditorium was filled three times a day, seven days a week. Before the younger group split off, this once-dynamic church was down to about 200 in attendance. After the split, only about twenty-five people were left.

Church splits are the opposite of Jesus' command to "love one another as I have loved you." The once vibrant church was a shell of its former power and glory. In many cities, some of the grand old churches have been turned into theaters or restaurants, and others have been demolished and replaced with office buildings or parking lots.

I went to Matthew with an idea. "Do you remember me saying the Lord told me I would one day pastor the Angelus Temple? Let's see if we can get a meeting with the leaders of the denomination, the Foursquare International, who own the building."

We both suspected the chances of getting them to listen to us were slim, but I called the people in charge, and they were willing to meet with us. The backstory is that our two denominations hadn't always been on the best terms, and I wondered how this history might affect our meeting. Matthew and I drove to their headquarters and walked into the meeting. I knew we probably wouldn't have much time to plead our case, so I got right into it: "Gentlemen, we have a problem and an opportunity. Our church has more people than we have room, and you have a great building with plenty of room. Together, we could do great things for the Lord. Wouldn't it be a wonderful witness—two Pentecostal denominations working together for the kingdom of God?" The plan was to get people saved at Angelus Temple and disciple them at the Dream Center.

They asked for some time to think, pray, and discuss the offer with their leaders. As we left the building, I was optimistic. However, after four months went by without hearing from them, I became discouraged. After a few more weeks, I gave up on my audacious plan of moving into the Angelus Temple. But then I got a call that they wanted to meet with us again.

This time they came over to the Dream Center. We met in a conference room we affectionately call our "war room." Paul Risser, their president, began, "We like your idea, but we have one condition." He paused long enough for my mind to race to figure out what the condition might be, and then he continued, "Pastor, we aren't interested in a short-term relationship. We want you to commit to staying there for the rest of your life."

I could hardly believe my ears. That's exactly what we wanted, but didn't think we should ask for a long-term agreement. They had another surprise: "We know the Angelus Temple is going to need renovations, so we're going to commit $8 million. We'll let you make all the design and decorating decisions."

This was far, far better than I could have imagined. They were giving us their historic church, and they were paying much of the bill to refurbish it. We would renovate the building with *their* money. It was an unprecedented example of working together for the glory of God.

We shook hands, and after they left I practically was walking on air. Then it dawned on me—the deal had to be approved by our denomination. I didn't know if they would approve of us partnering with the Foursquare denomination.

I quickly made a trip to Springfield, Missouri, headquarters of the Assemblies of God, and shared the exciting news with them. They listened intently and agreed that it made a lot of sense for us to take over the marvelous building. I was relieved, and then they asked about one minor little detail: "Will this be a Foursquare or an Assemblies of God church?"

I explained that it would technically be a Foursquare church and that Matthew, as lead pastor, would need to move his credentials to their denomination. It would be called "Dream Center Angelus Temple." After some discussion they agreed that the opportunity for ministry was too great to miss, so they agreed to the arrangement. Actually, this agreement had the wonderful effect of healing the wounds caused by the division that happened when Aimee McPherson was offended and left the Assemblies of God.

We had a lot of work to do to renovate the building. It had to meet current building codes, and we wanted it to look as magnificent as it did when it opened about sixty years before. Between the contractors and a lot of volunteer labor from the Dream Center, we finally were ready to move in. Matthew wanted me to preach the first service, or at least play a role in the grand opening, but I felt the focus needed to be entirely on the Lord, the church, and him. I would always be available to help him in any way, but when the church opened its doors, he would be the pastor.

More than 5,000 people showed up on the first Sunday morning, including Hollywood celebrities, residents from the neighborhood, civic leaders, Dream Center residents, executives from both denominations, men and women who were homeless, and people of all races and ethnicities. It was a picture of heaven joining together to celebrate God's goodness and worship the King of kings!

Today, Angelus Temple attracts approximately 8,000 people every week. We've grown the old-fashioned way—in my opinion, the only way to grow a church. We reach out to the people who live near the church, find a way to bring them in, and introduce them to Jesus. Some people drive long distances because they love the church, and some of them are famous. One Easter, Stevie Wonder unexpectedly came and asked if he could sing, and of course, we were thrilled. But the core of our church consists of ordinary people whose lives have been changed by the gospel. Our goal isn't to entertain people. We hope they feel inspired and welcomed so their hearts are open to the message of Jesus dying in our place so we can belong to Him. Soul winning isn't an option. It's a command. It's our privilege and responsibility to proclaim this message and model God's heart of love for every person.

God never makes mistakes. He told me one day I would be the pastor of Angeles Temple. As far as I'm concerned, He's made good on that promise.

WITH MARJA

CHAPTER 29

Our Secret Burden

*W*hen God called me into the ministry at a young age, he called me into one of the most rewarding and meaningful professions on earth. I don't think people who work in full-time Christian ministry are better than anyone else, but we've been given the opportunity to lead God's church, inviting people to accept Jesus and helping them grow in their faith. Even though every Christian is called to serve, I consider it a great privilege to do God's ministry as an evangelist and pastor for sixty-six years and counting. However, most people who serve in ministry agree that sometimes it seems like the enemy works overtime on us, usually by attacking our families. My kids—Kristie, Luke, and Matthew—have responded to the grace of God and have avoided the difficulties children of pastors can suffer. But another person paid a price for my commitment to ministry . . . the love of my life, Marja.

This is a story I'm reluctant to tell, but with Marja's urging, we've decided to share it. Actually, among pastor's wives, Marja's story is a familiar one. We hope that her vulnerability will validate the pain others experience and encourage them to get the help they need.

It all started with the Dream Center, the very thing that brought us so much joy and so many miraculous restorations. Something happened the night Marja learned that a man put a gun to Matthew's head: she experienced the first of many panic attacks. It was so frightening that we rushed her to the hospital.

If you haven't experienced a panic attack, it's much more than a temporary fear. It's a sudden episode of intense fear that includes a number of symptoms, such as a racing heart, sweating, trembling, dizziness, and shortness of breath. And worse than all of these is the terror of impending danger. All of us experience fear when something happens that triggers our response to danger, but when the stimulus is gone, the fear subsides. Panic attacks can happen without warning apart from any obvious stimulus, and they leave the person feeling deeply shaken, not relieved that the danger is over.

Imagine making breakfast on a beautiful spring morning when everything seems right with the world, and out of nowhere your heart starts beating like a jackhammer, sweat pours off your forehead, your hands and maybe your entire body is shaking, and you have trouble breathing. Eventually the physical symptoms fade, but not before your whole being is enveloped in a deep sense of foreboding. Something's wrong, but you don't know what. You're sure that something tragic is about to happen, but you don't know to whom or when. Then later in the day, or sometime the next day, or maybe after several days, it happens again. And again. And again. Far too often, the people around you don't understand, and they give simplistic answers to this deep and complex problem. That was what happened to Marja, and it was triggered by Matthew's experience.

At first, we assumed Marja's reaction was a response to Matthew serving in such a dangerous part of Los Angeles, but her symptoms continued even after receiving wonderful reports of the great things that were happening through his ministry. If anything, they got worse and became more frequent. I had no idea how to help her.

Of course, we prayed. Marja and I prayed together, and often our kids joined us in praying for her delivery from these attacks. I fully believe God heals. I've seen miraculous healings with my own eyes, and I've often prayed over the sick and seen them healed. But I also know that sometimes God chooses not to intervene in the way we would like Him to. It was clear that despite our prayers, Marja wasn't getting better.

I also believe God heals through science and medicine—knowledge that comes from Him in the first place—so we scheduled an appointment with our doctor. We learned that we weren't alone. In the United States, approximately eleven percent of the population has experienced a panic attack, and they tend to occur more in women than in men. In most cases, the panic attack is a singular event and may never happen again. But for some, they occur frequently, and the person becomes chronically afraid of having the next panic attack—a cycle of fear about fear. In these cases, the most common treatment is a prescription for an anti-anxiety medication.

Marja's doctor gave her a prescription for Xanax, a sedative that treats anxiety and panic attacks. Within a couple of weeks, Marja's panic attacks stopped. Just to be safe, our doctor told her to continue taking the medicine. His advice made sense to both of us because we didn't want the symptoms to return. It was agonizing to see her suffer so much from them. Soon, Marja began to laugh again. We were relieved that this difficult chapter had ended, but another was about to begin.

After a couple of months, her laughter subsided, and she appeared listless. I assumed she wasn't getting enough sleep. When she came to the kitchen table for breakfast, she just sat, sipping her coffee and not saying much. When I realized she was getting plenty of sleep, I assumed she was exhausted because she was taking on too many projects. One day I came home in the afternoon and found her still in bed, the bedroom shades closed to block out the light. "What's the matter, honey?" I asked. "Aren't you feeling well?"

She assured me she was fine and just needed to rest for a while. I knew that wasn't it. Marja and I talked about what was going on, and I realized she had developed a dependency on Xanax. By the time we realized what was happening, she was taking three times the prescribed dosage.

I didn't know what to do. I was committed to get Marja the help she needed, but I was the pastor of one of the largest congregations in America, and I was invited to speak at events all over the world. By now there were 900 residents living at the Dream Center, and we fed them and offered shelter at no cost to them. Matthew and I had to raise approximately $900,000 a month to keep the Dream Center going. I felt enormous pressure, and I searched for answers.

My solution was to keep quiet. I'm not proud of my reaction. I've thought about it many times.

I've learned that denial is the most common response to a family crisis. When we're immobilized by a combination of fear, denial, shame, and ignorance, we press on, hoping the problem will go away, or at least hoping nobody notices. I had plenty of distractions because everything in my ministry was going well. But I was torn between the pressing demands of ministry and Marja's tragic condition.

I've also learned that one person's problem with an addictive substance or behavior is the whole family's problem. Everyone is deeply affected, and everyone needs help. Almost always, a pattern of denial is combined with repressed emotions and unhealthy ways of trying to manage the stress. Marja needed help, and so did I.

I'd like to report that God miraculously delivered Marja, but it didn't happen. She didn't get better in a year . . . or two years . . . or three years. For fifteen years, Marja essentially dropped out of sight at the church as the kids and I continued in ministry. I'm sure the people from church wondered what was going on, but we were a big church, and the spotlight hadn't been on Marja. The church continued to grow. We initiated some of our most innovative programs to reach out to our community, and the Dream Center in Los Angeles received accolades from city officials. In addition, people were coming from all over the world to learn how to build their own Dream Centers. During all of this, Marja, the beautiful Swedish immigrant, devoted pastor's wife, and loving mother was fighting the battle of her life. We did our best to "put on a happy face" to those around us, feeling that they had enough problems of their own and didn't need to hear about ours.

After fifteen years, nothing had changed, and I realized we had to do something or we might lose Marja. According to the research, the longer someone uses Xanax, the greater the possibility of suicide. In one of our many meetings as a family to cope with what was happening, we decided we needed to have an intervention. We set a date, then prayed, asking God to prepare Marja's heart for what we needed to tell her.

That day in late November of 2008, the kids came over and we gathered in our living room. I went into the bedroom, helped Marja get out of bed, and led her down the hall and to the living room. When she saw the kids, she knew what was happening, and I could tell she wanted to run away. I asked her to sit and talk with us. She slumped onto the couch and stared straight ahead as each of our children quietly spoke.

"Mom, I love you so much. I know you're hurting, and we just want you to get help."

"Mom, you've always been there for us when we were sick or discouraged. Now it's our turn. We love you."

"You used to be so much fun. Always the life of the party and helping everyone else have a good time. I want that mom back. Please let us find you the help you need."

It was a precious, sacred time. There were tears and a lot of hugs, and it was clear that Marja was moved by the love and courage of her kids. We ended by gathering around her, laying our hands on her, and praying that God would walk with her through the journey we wanted her to take.

The next day, she reluctantly packed a small suitcase, and I took her to one of the finest rehabilitation centers in America. I knew she didn't want to spend the required two months there, and I was proud of her for agreeing to go. After going through the admission process, I gave her a big hug and a kiss and watched her walk through a set of large doors into a brightly lit corridor. She looked so frail and alone as she walked through those doors. It broke my heart, but I knew that this was the right thing to do. With powerful and mixed emotions, I got back in my car to drive home. I was filled with hope that when I returned to pick her up, I would have the *real* Marja back.

When I got home, I walked into an empty house. Even though Marja had retreated to her bedroom all those years, at least she was there. I called the kids to let them know how things had gone and asked them to come over. I needed to have them near me for a little while, but I also wanted to run an idea by them: "I think we need to tell the church."

Those words got their attention. After some discussion, we decided I would announce it the next Sunday.

ANNOUNCING MARJA'S ROAD
TO RECOVERY BEFORE CHRISTMAS

CHAPTER 30

Going Public

I'm not sure there's ever a "right time" to tell a church about a family member's substance abuse, but this seemed like a very strange time to make the announcement. The next Sunday night was the beginning of our 2008 Christmas pageant, and as always, we were pulling out all the stops. It featured a full orchestra, state-of-the-art technology, and special effects that rival anything on Broadway.

I had a heavy heart as I sat in my office before the opening night of the pageant. In a few minutes I would share something incredibly personal and private about our family. I had already told the board, and Marja wanted me to share her struggles with our church, but it was an announcement I didn't want to make. I tried rehearsing exactly what I should say. How about this? "Dear friends, it's with a heavy heart that I come to you with the news that my wife Marja is experiencing a serious health issue for which we covet your prayers."

I rationalized that this was, in fact, truthful and would maintain some privacy for us because people generally don't ask a lot of questions when you mention a "health issue." Yes, it was truthful, but not the whole truth.

I struggled to come up with a statement that used words like "prescription drugs" and "dependency" and "rehabilitation." I decided the best course was to just tell the truth.

At the close of the service while people were standing, many at the altar, I walked up to the pulpit and began. "Some of you may have been wondering why you haven't seen much of Marja." The place got very quiet. "Several years ago, Marja began having panic attacks. Our doctor ordered a prescription for Xanax, and she subsequently developed a dependency. I have taken her to a rehabilitation facility where she will receive treatment for the next two months. Please pray for Marja. I love her, and I know you do, too."

I received tremendous affirmation and support that night. We got numerous cards and notes from people assuring us of their prayers and love for us. It was truly overwhelming, but it shouldn't have surprised me because compassion is woven into our church's DNA. It's what we practice as the body of Christ, but somehow I had forgotten that it also applied to Marja. Too many times, people in ministry think everything has to be perfect in their lives, and when it isn't, they pretend it is. Our lack of honesty causes us to miss the blessings God wants to give us during difficult times. I'm so grateful for our church.

After two months at the rehabilitation facility, I picked Marja up. I could hardly believe the change. For the first time in more than fifteen years, I saw glimpses of my Marja when she was happy and healthy. She smiled and talked all the way home, and her radiance had returned. Our kids were there when we got home, and we gathered around Marja for a wonderful time of prayer. We thanked God for the victory we can experience and the obvious fact that God had delivered her! She has been free of her dependency since then. Now when I come home, the shades are wide open.

You can understand why I didn't want to share this story. This was a painful time in our lives, and revisiting it hasn't been easy for any of us, but I opened the window to it for a reason. Over the years I've learned that a lot of pastors' wives (as well as pastors and their children) struggle with dependency to prescription drugs, alcohol, or other substances—and just as we did, they've struggled alone.

For fifteen years, we kept our secret because we were too embarrassed and ashamed. We didn't want anyone to know that we had a problem, which is ridiculous because *all of us* have problems. Our story isn't unique, especially for families in ministry. And all of us can get the help we need.

I sometimes wonder *what if*. What if the man hadn't pulled a gun on Matthew? What if the doctor hadn't prescribed the addictive medication? What if I had been more assertive in getting help sooner? What if, what if, what if. These questions are normal, but they're not productive. In the sovereignty and grace of God, He acted to give us wisdom and courage in His timing, and He brought good out of great difficulty.

Thank God, I have my precious wife back. Every night when I get home, she's ready to go. We may go exercise together, or go shopping together, enjoy a nice meal together, or hike in the mountains together. If we can find a good movie, we go together. No matter what we do, we do it together. We're making up for the lost years, and it's wonderful.

PREPARING FOR A NIGHT ON THE
STREETS OF SKID ROW

CHAPTER 31

Renewing the Vision

*I*n 2009 on the fifteenth anniversary of the Dream Center, Matthew came to me and said, "Dad, you and I need to do something to keep us fresh." He was afraid caring for hurting people would become too routine and we'd lose the heart of what God wants us to do. I've heard that attorneys don't want doctors or pastors on juries because they've seen so much pain that they can become desensitized to it. Matthew and I didn't want that to happen to us, so we came up with a plan. After the Thursday night of the anniversary celebration, we were going to live on the streets for a night and a day. Both of us dressed up (or actually, down) in worn-out jeans, ragged shirts, stocking caps, and old shoes. We let our beards grow for a few days. (We looked like most worship leaders today!) We didn't take any money. The only thing we carried were large pieces of cardboard like the ones used for kitchen appliances. We needed these to keep us off the ground at night.

That night we had someone drop us off a few blocks from Skid Row in downtown Los Angeles. Matthew went in one direction, and I went another. I walked to the area where hundreds of tents sheltered street people. Among the gleaming, beautiful buildings of the financial district, the homeless set up their tents and wander the streets and parks. One of the streets has attracted people who are dying of HIV-AIDS. On all the streets you'll find women known as "strawberries," who go from tent to tent having sex for a few dollars, and sometimes less than a dollar, so they can buy their next hit of heroin or some other drug.

Matthew and I planned to meet at noon the next day. In the first hour or so, numerous women offered sex, and it didn't take long for a man to dangle a little bag of either cocaine or heroin in front of me. (I didn't ask what it was.) I wanted to find out how the system works. He asked me for $20, but I shook my head. He said, "Okay, I'll take $15." Again, I motioned that his price was too high. He looked frustrated, but he offered it to me for $10. For the third time, I said, "Sorry. That's too much." He said, "Alright, you can have it for $5." I turned and walked away, but I learned that these people will do anything for money to support their drug or alcohol addiction.

By about midnight, the area was lit by more than street lights—a number of people built bonfires out of the trash in dozens of trash-cans. The police drove slowly by and just watched. Soon, I found a place outside a store to put down my cardboard so I could get some sleep, but the owner of the store opened the door and began hosing off the sidewalk. I found another spot nearby and again thought it was a good place to sleep. A few minutes later from my ground-level view, I saw a colony of huge rats scurrying about fifty feet away. I got out of there in a hurry.

Midnight Mission has a fenced area where they allow street people to sleep, so I found my way there. The place was packed like a tin of sardines, but I found a little space to lie down. I tried to sleep, but the smell of the people near me was so strong that I didn't sleep at all. After a long while, I looked at the man next to me. Even in the dim light, I could tell he was old, filthy, and covered in sores. The thought hit me: *It was for this man that Jesus died.* At about 4:00 in the morning, someone came out the door of the mission and told us, "You'll have to leave now. We need to get breakfast ready."

As soon as I walked through the gate, a pickup truck arrived and stopped. Some ladies got out and gave food to everyone who was hungry, which was all of us. It was the best burrito I've ever tasted! Later I discovered that these dear ladies worked at a restaurant. They took the leftovers and made them into burritos for the people living on the street. This was real ministry . . . and real love.

Before dawn, I struck up a conversation with a teenage boy who was about six-feet six-inches tall and weighed close to 300 pounds. He told me he was from San Diego, and he had run away from home. I told him that I'd had trouble finding a place to sleep, and he whispered, "Follow me." He led me down a number of streets to a wooded area near an overpass. He told me, "The police won't find us here." Suddenly, I realized he might have more than sleep on his mind. I was afraid he would hit me in the head. His motive couldn't have been money because it was obvious I didn't have any. Still, I sensed danger, so I made an excuse and got out of there!

Later that morning, a young woman approached me. As we talked, I blew my cover. I said, "You don't belong here. Do you know about the Dream Center?" She nodded. She said she had seen the white Dream Center buses that drive to Skid Row to pick people up for every service. I explained, "If you'll come to the Dream Center, we'll give you a nice place to live, feed you, and help you get your GED and training for a good job. It won't cost you a penny." I told her I'd meet her at a certain place at 10:00 the next morning so a bus could pick her up.

Matthew had a similar encounter with a young woman who offered herself to him for a few dollars. As he started talking with her, she burst into tears, "Oh, Pastor Matthew! I'm so sorry!" Sometime before that night, she had gone in one of our buses to a service at the Dream Center, and now she recognized him. He encouraged her to come back to the Dream Center where she would find the help she needed.

On Saturday morning, I went to the place where I was going to meet the young girl I'd met, but she wasn't there. I went with Matthew to the spot where he had agreed to meet the young woman he had talked with, and she was there! I'm not sure who was the most excited, Matthew, me, or her. We rode with her, and we praised the Lord for her willingness to get help.

After introducing her to the staff, Matthew and I went back to the streets. We planned to panhandle that morning to see what these people experience. Again, we split up. He went downtown, and I found my way to the entrance of a freeway where I'd often seen people with signs asking for money. I made a sign that said, "Hungry. Need money for food." The truth is that I was genuinely hungry, and I gave the money to the Dream Center to buy food, so I was telling the truth on both counts. I was there for about forty-five minutes, and people gave me a total of $16. Matthew must have been new to the fine art of panhandling because he went into a restricted area and almost got arrested and put in jail! And he only raised $5, so next time he'll need to take lessons from me.

My few days on the street vividly illustrated a number of lessons for me, but one of the clearest is that it's very difficult to find a good place to sleep on the streets. People can be run off by store owners, rats the size of small dogs, the police, and the smell of people who have lost so much dignity that they don't bother to bathe.

Later that Saturday, a van picked us up to take us back. We had lived on the street for only a day and a night, but it had accomplished its purpose. As soon as I sat in the backseat, I started weeping. A flood of memories from the past couple of days reminded me how much these people need tangible expressions of God's love. Like them, I felt belittled and despised. Some of the people I passed by on the street wouldn't even look at me. I had become invisible to them. A lady stopped when I was panhandling near the freeway and held out a $5 bill. I assured her I wasn't going to buy drugs, but she cursed at me and yelled, "I don't care what you do with the money!" I wondered then—and I still wonder now—what would motivate someone to give, but with such contempt. It just doesn't make sense to me. But some people, like the ladies in the pickup who brought burritos to us, have hearts like Jesus, full of compassion and generosity. That's the kind of person I want to be. That's the kind of church I want to lead. That's the kind of impact I want to have on cities. That's the kind of heart I want to see God multiply in the lives of leaders all over this country and around the world. That's the character and nature of Jesus. He invited us to follow Him wherever He leads . . . and He always leads us to care for the poor and needy.

ON THE 736 MILE RUN TO LA TO RAISE
MONEY FOR THE LA DREAM CENTER

CHAPTER 32

Running Far, Running Over

*I*n late 2010, I didn't feel well—which was unusual for me because I've always been very healthy—so I scheduled an appointment with my doctor. He listened to my chest and said he thought I might have pneumonia. He sent me to the hospital for some tests, which included an MRI. It was my first one, and I hope it's the last. It was very unpleasant—and not just because they make you wear a skimpy gown. The technician instructed me to lie down on a long table, and he told me to remain perfectly still. He quickly left the room, and then the table began to slide into a narrow tube until I was surrounded in the tight enclosure. It felt like I'd been stuffed into a soda straw—I felt more than a little claustrophobic! After a while, the table slid out of the tube. After the MRI, the technician came in and told me not to move a muscle while a doctor examined the MRI results.

After a little while, a young doctor came in and immediately asked, "Has anyone ever told you that you have a leaky valve in your heart?"

That sounded ominous, but what came next really scared me. "We're going to have to schedule you for open-heart surgery."

I couldn't believe it. I'd always been active, and I loved playing sports with my boys. I was a runner, even using the sport to raise money for the Dream Center and baptize a Native American. Let me explain. On my sixtieth birthday, I preached the evening service wearing my workout clothes. I explained that after the service I would begin a 436-mile "Race Across the Desert" to raise money for the Dream Center. I invited anyone who was interested to join me. When the service was over, I raced down the aisle and just about everybody followed me as the theme song from *Rocky* blasted over the sound system. Of course, they didn't wear their running clothes, so after a half mile, only Marja and I were running. We ran a few miles and spent the night at a hotel on the outskirts of Phoenix.

The next morning, I woke up at 5:00 a.m., laced up my running shoes as Marja slept, and left a note on the door: "Catch me if you can!" I covered thirty-five miles that day, and it just about killed me. The next morning, I felt a lot better and was ready for another day on the road. As I pounded the dirt road through an Indian reservation, I noticed a man in a pickup truck following me. After a while, he pulled up beside me and asked, "Where ya going?"

"Los Angeles," I responded.

He looked puzzled. "What for?"

"Because I'm raising money to buy a place where we can treat people who are addicted to alcohol and drugs, people who are experiencing serious problems."

Tears came to his eyes and he told me, "Sounds like the kind of place I need."

He introduced himself as James, and I could tell he was a Native American. He explained that he had been an athlete—he was such a gifted basketball player that he was known as "the Native-American

Michael Jordan." James had gotten involved in drugs and was facing a long prison sentence. As he shared his story with me, I kept running. Soon, my support car driver, Gary, pulled up and joined the conversation.

"Gary," I said as I winked at him, "this guy needs someone to talk to."

Gary knew that my wink meant that James needed the Lord. As I ran on, Gary and James pulled over to the side of the road. As I ran down the long, straight road, I looked back a few times, and they were still there. After a while, I lost sight of them. A few minutes later, James pulled up in his truck. I could already see the change in his face. Gary had led him to the Lord. I stopped to hear his story. He got out of his truck, and Gary soon joined us. We praised God for what He had done for James. James and Gary got back in their trucks, and I started running again. I was only a little way down the road when James leaned out of his window and yelled, "Hey, Pastor, I want to get baptized!"

I turned and told him, "That's great, James. Just stop by our church, and we'll be happy to baptize you."

"But you don't understand," he answered. "I'll be in prison. I need to get baptized right now."

"That's impossible, James. We're out here in the middle of the desert. There's no water."

Gary walked back to his car and grabbed a bottle of water and handed it to me. I wanted to laugh, but this was a sacred moment. I told him, "Okay, James. Stick your head out the window." I poured water over his head and baptized him in the name of the Father, the Son, and the Holy Ghost . . . Methodist style.

Over the next nineteen days, I averaged a marathon a day—26.2 miles. My blisters developed blisters, and my feet swelled from size nine to size twelve. Eventually I made it to Los Angeles, arriving at

AT THE FINISH LINE OF THE FUND-RAISING RUN TO LA

Grauman's Chinese Theatre. I was greeted by celebrities like Dyan Cannon and Lou Rawls, a host of other Hollywood stars who attended church at the Dream Center, pastors from all over the country who had flown in for the occasion, and people from our church. Hundreds of them ran with me as I continued down Hollywood Boulevard to Sunset Boulevard and then a few more blocks to the Dream Center. I was physically spent, but got a second wind when more than 2,000 people threw confetti as I crossed the finish line at the Dream Center. It was grueling, but it was worth it. The run raised $750,000 to help pay for Queen of Angels Hospital.

I'm a runner—that's why I was so surprised at the doctor's diagnosis that something was wrong with my heart. Of course, the doctor

Religion

Fund Drive for $2 Million Starts With Single Step

■ **Run:** Phoenix pastor had always wished to see more of the country. L.A. center needed money for repairs. His 400-mile journey combined both goals.

By VALERIE BURGHER
TIMES STAFF WRITER

Over the last three weeks, the Rev. Tommy Barnett performed a baptism with a bottle of Evian, prayed with boxer Evander Holyfield, and discovered that his true shoe size is not 9½ but 11—all while running from Phoenix to Los Angeles.

Barnett, an Assembly of God minister based in Phoenix, cele-

the money needed to keep the church's Los Angeles International Center in Echo Park from closing.

Barnett and other Assembly of God leaders started the center

addictions. The center, which is run by Barnett's 23-year-old son, Matthew, is staffed by 200 volunteers and provides housing, food, job counseling and religious services.

Los Angeles city officials said

Barnett said he has longed for a cross-country run since growing up as a pastor's son in the Midwest. "I used to think about running across America, although no one was doing it at the time. To do it now made a set

The Rev. Tommy Barnett, with wife, Marja, and actress Dyan Cannon, leaves Mann's Chinese Theatre

LUIS SINCO / Los Angeles Times

MARJA AND DYAN CANNON WITH ME AT THE GRAUMAN CHINESE THEATER

who reviewed my MRI didn't know anything about this exploit. He scheduled surgery for the day after our Pastors School, which, ironically, was Valentine's Day. I was shocked! I shared the news with the pastors, and we had a wonderful service as they gathered around me to pray. When I checked in to the hospital, a group of pastors and men from the church came and prayed for me. It was so comforting to have this kind of support, but I had no idea how much I would need it.

On Valentine's Day, 2011, I went under the knife. The surgery was successful, but no one told me that many heart surgery patients experience severe depression during their recovery. For the next four months, I was deeply depressed and filled with fear. I had never in my life experienced anything like it. Like Marja years before, I shut the blinds on the windows, fearful that someone would break into our house. I couldn't watch television because the news and every other program scared me. I was so depressed that I didn't want to leave the house or see anybody. In fact, I had no interest in ministry and no desire to do anything at all. I might have just given up if it hadn't been for my family and a lot of loving, caring people. Let me mention two of them.

One of the laymen from our church had run into some trouble several years prior to my depression, and I helped him get through it. He was excited about the Lord and became one of the most generous supporters in our church. When I felt hopeless, he stopped by every week to encourage me. He listened to me share my doubts and fears, and he assured me, "Someday God is going to allow you to do greater things for Him than you ever imagined. You're going to do things around the world that you never thought you could do."

Charles Nieman also reached out to me. He pastored a church that almost shut down when news of the Jim Bakker scandal broke. People were hurt, confused, and angry—not just at Jim Bakker, but at any Christian leader near them, leaders like Charles. A trickle of people leaving his church turned into a flood, and Charles became very discouraged. He had no idea what to do. I knew him to be a gifted leader and a devoted man of God. I met with him, prayed with him, and did my best to encourage him, and he claimed that my support changed his life. Today, Abundant Living Faith Center in El Paso, Texas, averages around 20,000—it's one of America's great churches. When he learned I wasn't doing well, he flew to Phoenix every other week just to be with me. Each time, he told me what I really didn't want to hear: "You're going to get through this, and your ministry will grow more than ever!"

The consistent, encouraging, hopeful messages from these men turned out to be true. I didn't believe them at the time, but I should have. They were illustrating a principle I had taught throughout my ministry: whatever you want to receive, you have to give away. This principle is, of course, entirely counterintuitive to people in our culture. The vast majority of people believe that we need to grab and hoard as much as possible. But Jesus said, "Give and it will be given to you." Whenever you invest in others, it will come back to you in abundance, or, as Jesus put it, "running over."

When I was depressed, I had no idea how God might restore me and expand my ministry, but I soon found out.

WITH LUKE AND MATTHEW

CHAPTER 33

Team Tommy

Gradually, the depression began to lift as the Holy Spirit helped me overcome the intense fear that had me in its grip. With the encouragement of my family and dear friends, I finally could see the light at the end of the tunnel—and it wasn't an approaching freight train like I'd thought! Something else began to lift my spirits. In my absence from the pulpit, my son Luke, who had served as one of my associate pastors, stepped in for me. Immediately, I heard reports that the church was thriving under his leadership. I was thrilled! One of my worries was that the church would falter without me. Their continued growth was a tribute to a wonderful church, Luke's passion for ministry, and the powerful anointing on his life.

My return to ministry happened when I officiated at my granddaughter's wedding. I was overjoyed to see this beautiful young lady walk down the aisle, and the experience convinced me that I was ready to get back in the saddle. It was obvious, though, that I needed to begin thinking about a transition. One of the biggest challenges facing large churches is pastoral succession. I had been the senior pastor in Phoenix for thirty-five years and led it through good times and bad. I was fortunate to enjoy strong support from my board and the congregation. I wasn't ready to walk away, but I knew God soon would have other things for me to do.

Conversations with the board confirmed our direction for the transition, and they named Luke as the Lead Pastor. It was a natural choice. Luke is a gifted preacher as well as a natural leader. He can relate to the affluent, but he also has a heart for the poor. He and his wife, Angel, are a terrific team, and they have a special gift of caring for those in need.

One of my first Sundays back, I explained to the church that the board had named Luke the Lead Pastor, and I would remain as Senior Pastor. With Luke as Lead Pastor, I would have more time to raise funds for the Dream Center and still preach to the congregation I loved. When I announced the change to the church, they responded with a standing ovation. In fact, this arrangement worked out so well that after a year, I felt Luke should be appointed Senior Pastor, and my title would change to Global Pastor, allowing me to teach and preach at churches around the world as they reach their nations for the Lord.

Several years ago, the late Bill Bright, founder of Campus Crusade, handed me a baton—the type used in relay races at track meets. Inscribed on that aluminum baton were the words: "To reach a billion souls for Christ." It was a goal I've taken seriously, and by stepping away from the day-to-day activities of our church, I have been able to pursue this challenging assignment.

To make the change official, I called Luke up to the platform and announced that he would be the Senior Pastor. I then pulled that baton out of my pocket and handed it to him. We had a marvelous time of prayer. The church rallied around him, accepting their new leader and giving me their blessing to pursue new dreams that God was giving me.

Luke continues to amaze me in the way he's grown the church in Phoenix, which we now call Dream City Church. Under his

LUKE'S FAMILY: ANNALEE, LUKE, AUBREY,
ASH, AND ANGEL

leadership, thousands come to the Pastors & Leaders School, now called the Dream Conference. One of the most important additions to Dream City Church is our Prayer Pavilion of Light. We built this gleaming building on the side of the mountain uphill from the church. It has a 250-seat chapel where people pray twenty-four hours a day, seven days a week. They get there by taking a 200-yard walk through the desert landscape and find three garden courtyards and a 50-foot cross. When people in the city of Phoenix look at our church, they see a bold display of our commitment to prayer.

Matthew, along with his wife Caroline, continue to lead the Los Angeles Dream Center and pastor the Angelus Temple. Every week, they reach approximately 50,000 people with the life-giving message

Photo by Bill Timmerman, debartolo architects

PRAYER PAVILION OF LIGHT

of the gospel, whether it's through sheltering victims of human trafficking, feeding the hungry, or preaching to a packed auditorium of rich and poor, people from all over the world, celebrities and homeless, Christians and curious.

To help raise money for the Dream Center, Matthew is living proof that the apple doesn't fall far from the tree. In 2017, he participated in the World Marathon Challenge—that's seven marathons in seven days on seven continents. While the other thirty-two participants competed for a trophy, Matt used this grueling event to raise money for the Dream Center. They started in Antarctica, then traveled to Chile, Miami, Madrid, Morocco, Dubai, and Sydney. In Morocco he severely injured his leg and had to limp during the final two races.

MATTHEW'S FAMILY:
MIA, CAROLINE, CADEN AND MATTHEW

On the plane to Sydney, he had to be given IV fluids, but he finished all seven marathons—and raised $1.6 million for the Dream Center.[4]

It seems the running gene has been passed to Matthew's daughter Mia, who is currently in high school and has one of the fastest miles in the country. (As you can tell, I'm a proud grandfather!) His next goal is to shoot 50,000 free throws—one for every homeless person in Los Angeles—to raise money for the Dream Center. I'm not sure where he gets these crazy ideas.

---

4 You can read more about it here: http://www.espn.com/sports/endurance/story/_/id/18638941/pastor-matthew-barnett-lives-tell-2017-world-marathon-challenge

One of my favorite stories about Matthew happened when a man in his church ran up to him and said, "There's a man out here who claims to be Jesus! What do you want me to do?"

Instantly Matthew told him, "Bring him in. I want to meet him."

A few minutes later, the man brought "Jesus" through the doors and toward Matthew. He wore a white robe and had long, flowing white hair and beard. Matthew held out his hand and said, "It's good to meet you. What's your name?"

He solemnly replied, "I am Jesus Christ of Nazareth, the Son of the Living God."

Matthew introduced himself, and then he asked, "Did you ever see *The Passion of the Christ*?"

He frowned and shook his head, "No, I couldn't stand to watch it. The movie brings back too many bad memories."

Rounding out "Team Tommy" is my lovely daughter, Kristie Sexton. I've said this often—Kristie could do anything Matthew and Luke have done, and maybe even better. (I'll probably hear from the boys on that one.) She's an accomplished speaker and a leader, having spoken in churches at home and abroad. She has a gift for ministering to women and leads an exercise ministry in our church called "Kristie's Bootcamp." It's free because Kristie knows that many women can't afford to join a health club. And it's tough—she really whips them into shape! But Kristie has always felt her first calling was to be a wife to Kent and a mom to Chantelle, Chase, and Kent, Jr. She and Kent have built a successful business, which enables them to provide generous financial support for a number of ministries. She is presently leading a walk-a-thon with a goal of 10,000 participants to raise $1 million dollars for women caught in sex trafficking. When people meet Kristie and get to know her, they always say she reminds them of me, and I take that as a high compliment.

CHANTELLE, KENT JR. HOLDING MY GREAT GRANDSON
EVAN, KRISTIE, KENT, TOMMY CHASE, AND TAYLOR

When I see the way my kids are serving the Lord and think back on that little pump house in Electra, Texas, I almost have to pinch myself. I guess my dad was right when he told me that if I just preached that Jesus saves, I'll be just fine. Actually, my understanding of God's grace has grown as I've realized that the gospel covers every need. That's a message for all of us. Jesus told us that if we seek Him first, all we need will be given to us. The legacy continues, from my father to me, from me to my children, and now from our children to our grandchildren who are walking with the Lord and many of whom are serving in ministry.

He also told us not to worry about tomorrow, but what about the past?

THE WORLD'S LARGEST SNOW CONE

CHAPTER 34

No Regrets?

hen we host the Pastors & Leaders School, we have a session when several hundred people can ask me any question that's on their minds. One recurring question was recently voiced by a pastor: "Pastor Barnett, what's the secret of your success?" After a pause, he explained, "I feel like you haven't been completely forthcoming." After another second or two, he had the courage to say what he really wanted to say, "Pastor, you're not the greatest theologian, you're not the most gifted preacher, your voice—I'm sorry to tell you this—isn't the most charming, and you're not the handsomest guy I've ever seen. Come on, tell us your secret."

I smiled and said, "Shut up and sit down! Next question?" All of us had a good laugh, but it's a perfectly reasonable (and accurate) assessment, and a very good question. Actually, he only voiced part of my deficiencies. I've written twelve books, but I'm certainly not a gifted author; I've never taken a course in social work, but I've played a role in establishing Dream Centers that care for the poor, sick, and needy all over the world; I've never completed college, much less a doctorate, but I'm the chancellor of two great universities. (I'm glad he didn't mention those!)

On another of these occasions, a pastor's question caught me off guard. He asked, "As you look over your life, is there anything you would do differently?"

I'm sure plenty of people have wrestled with their answer. I had to think about it for a long time because I don't live in the past. I don't spend much time looking back because there are so many things I want to do in the future. General Douglas MacArthur once said that you can tell if a man is young or old by whether he looks for the sunrise or the sunset. I'm a sunrise kind of guy, so it was hard for me to think back over my life to identify any regrets—to consider what I might have done differently if I could live my life over again. Still, it was a good exercise, one that everyone should do every decade or so. I thought long and hard to determine if I had any regrets, and I found a few.

First, I would dream bigger dreams and take bigger risks. In every dream for ministry that I've had and every risk that I've taken, God did exceedingly and abundantly more than anything I could ask for or think. When God called me to be a preacher, my dream was to build a great church. How big was that dream? 7,000. That's how many showed up to hear Charles Fuller preach the day my dad took me to hear him. God took that dream and tripled it—more than 21,000 attend the Dream City Church in Phoenix, Scottsdale, Glendale, Colorado, Omaha, and the Phoenix Dream Center. On some of our Palm Sunday and Easter Sunday services, we've ministered to as many as 50,000!

When Matthew tried to convince me that we should buy an ancient, run-down hospital, I was certain we'd never be able to afford it. When God came through for us, my dream was to build a center for the hurting people in our Los Angeles neighborhood. I remembered the hundredfold promise God gave me, and He multiplied *that* dream by almost 300—and maybe more because almost every week we learn of another Dream Center being opened somewhere in the world.

Then, when God planted the dream about the Angeles Temple, I almost laughed out loud. "God, You're really missing it on this one—they're Foursquare and I'm Assemblies of God, and we have no dealings with each other." My son is now the pastor there. Thankfully, God made it happen despite the fact that even in my wildest dreams I couldn't imagine it. To me, pastoring that church was out of the question—so impossible that I didn't even consider it.

I'm certainly grateful for all that God has accomplished, but it makes me wonder: If I had dared to dream even bigger dreams, how many more people would have trusted in the Lord? I've discovered that His plan for us is always bigger and better than ours. As I look back on my life, I'm both shocked and grateful—I never dreamed God would use me the way He has. I believe God wants us to dream big and ask big. When we abide in Him, Jesus said repeatedly, we can ask whatever we want and it will be done for us. But when we abide in Him—when we soak up His love, forgiveness, and power—our "wanter" changes, and we long for His glory, not ours, His kingdom, not ours, and His display of power and love, not ours. If we long for Him more than our popularity, power, or pleasure, we can genuinely pray, "Your kingdom come, Your will be done on earth as it is in heaven." God's plan is far bigger than anything we can imagine, and His will is far better than anything our minds can fathom.

It's popular to develop five-year goals and ten-year goals, but I've never done that because I think it limits God. As I look back on my ministry, from a human perspective it might seem like I was pretty bold (or even reckless) in what I've attempted to do to bring people to Jesus, but now I wonder if I should have set my sights even higher. A lot of people in ministry are like the disciples who saw the boy with the fish and loaves, looked at the huge crowd, and said to each other,

GOING UP IN THE RAPTURE

"How are we going to feed all these people with such a tiny basket of food? This will never work. Maybe we should send them home." It's easy to be a pessimist and find plenty of reasons something won't work, but God wants to do great things with our meager resources. We only need to be willing to set our sights higher than we think is humanly possible and trust God to do what only He can do.

Do you have a dream to do something wonderful to the glory of God? Multiply it by two right now. Then maybe by four tomorrow.

My second regret is my failure to finish college. I've often wondered if the lack of training has been a hindrance to my ministry. Over the years I've regretted this hole in my training because I wonder if it has limited my ministry. It's made me uncomfortable, especially when I meet with brilliant professors who astound me with their intellect . . . and I don't have a clue what they're talking about. Maybe I could have been a better pastor if I had stayed in college. Incredibly, God opened the door for me to become the chancellor of Grand Canyon University, a Baptist university that has more than 20,000 resident students at their Phoenix campus and another 100,000 online. And now, I'm chancellor at another wonderful school, Southeastern University, one of the largest Pentecostal universities in the world. In addition, SEU's President, Dr. Kent Ingle, and the school have named the College of Ministry & Theology in my honor. I'm humbled and deeply grateful.

Today more than ever, those interested in serving the Lord in professional ministry need to get *at least* a college or Bible school education. I know the Bible pretty well from reading it every day and studying it carefully, but I've never been able to read it in its original Hebrew and Greek languages like ministry students today. I've given my best counsel to people struggling with problems, but today's problems are so deep and complicated that courses in psychology and biblical counseling would be a valuable asset for any young preacher. When young people feel the call of God to ministry, we need to encourage them to get a good, solid, biblically based education.

For any reflective person, it's impossible to live without any regrets. After all, we're human. Too many people, however, keep looking back at the mistakes they've made and become so filled with regret that they can't see the blessings God has for them today. The good news is that God can use our mistakes to teach us important lessons, as I learned one Saturday many years ago when the phone rang.

The voice on the line was frantic: "Pastor, where *are* you? The funeral was supposed to start a half-hour ago."

A family who didn't attend our church in Phoenix lost their husband and father, and they asked me to hold his funeral. To my horror, I had completely forgotten about it. At that time in my ministry, the church couldn't afford to hire a secretary who would have reminded me. It would take me at least a half-hour to get to the church, and I couldn't make this poor family wait any longer, so I asked my associate who was at the church to officiate at the funeral. I felt awful about it. After the service, I contacted the family to apologize, but it was clear that my failure had hurt them deeply. The next Sunday, they came to our church and sat near the front, and every time I looked their way I could see the pain in their eyes. I couldn't blame them, but I also couldn't let my horrible mistake interfere with God's ministry. I made the mistake, and I apologized, and it was time to move on. Eventually, they forgave me—and I learned an important lesson about paying attention to my calendar.

Don't beat yourself up if you look back and see some things you wish you'd have done differently. The enemy will do his best to use your regrets to keep you discouraged, defeated, preoccupied with failure, and ashamed. The Apostle Paul offers us a beautiful and practical example of how to respond to blemishes in our past: "But one thing I do: forgetting what lies behind and straining forward to what lies ahead, I press on toward the goal for the prize of the upward call of God in Christ Jesus" (Philippians 3:13–14 ESV). Learn from your regrets, try not to make the same mistakes, but more importantly, look ahead to the opportunities God will give you if you remain faithful to Him.

PREACHING AT DREAM CITY CHURCH

PHOENIX DREAM CENTER

CHAPTER 35

The Center of My Dreams

*P*eople often ask when I'm going to retire. Billy Graham used to say that the word *retirement* isn't in the Bible, and that's my perspective, too. A few years ago, I had an issue with my heart, and after the surgeon fixed it, I concluded, "I need a new dream." As I thought and prayed about my next dream, the Lord impressed on me that my next dream should be to help others reach *their* dreams. That's what I'm doing, and I'm having a blast.

For example, our church in Phoenix had always reached out to the community to help people in need, but we were running into some logistical problems. In 2006, we had rented a big warehouse as a residence for homeless people, but the city shut us down because the area wasn't zoned for this purpose. We also tried housing girls who were being trafficked in homes that we either bought or rented, and again, the city told us we had to stop. One of the biggest challenges in trying to help hurting people is the NIMBY syndrome: "We're glad you're helping those people, just *not in my back yard.*"

During that time, a small group of members approached me with a dream of their own—they wanted to start a Dream Center in Phoenix. How thrilling it is to see God giving others a big, impossible dream! We started by driving one of our church buses around the city as we looked for a building that would meet our needs. Eventually, we found a four-story Embassy Suites Hotel that had closed and was for sale. We checked with the city and learned that the zoning regulations in that part of town would allow us to serve disadvantaged people. The owners were asking $7.5 million. We offered $4.9 million, and once again, we were surprised when they accepted it. Within a year, we were able to pay off the loan. Just as we did in Los Angeles, we began renovating the building floor by floor. In a way, our buildings in Los Angeles and now Phoenix illustrate our strategic plans: we take something run down, broken, or worn out and turn it into something beautiful. By the grace of God and the generosity of many people, we've expanded to several campuses.

Initially, we provided housing for sixty people who were either homeless or struggling with addiction. We fed another 300 homeless people on the streets every day. And this ministry grew; today, we house 350 people and serve another 36,000 in the community each month.

PHOENIX DREAM CENTER

PROVIDING SAFETY AND SHELTER

One of those we've helped is a man named Luke, an Iraq War veteran who found it difficult to cope when he returned to civilian life. As a boy, he was raised by a single mom, but he can't remember a time when she wasn't taking drugs. He joined the military to get away from that life, but he fell into it himself and found himself a half step away from utter hopelessness. He explained, "I knew I would probably die if I didn't get help, so I thought maybe I'd give this God thing a try. I came here and committed to a thirty-day program, accepted Christ, and eventually earned a college degree." Luke Meredith is now the Chief Strategy Officer at the Dream Center.

Brian Steele, the executive director of the Phoenix Dream Center, has taken this ministry farther than I dreamed was possible. Shortly after coming on board, he and his wife Skye began riding with the police on their nightly patrols. They were deeply moved when they saw young girls being forced to sell their bodies. They launched a program to get the girls off the streets and took the rescue ministry to a higher level. They worked with a building contractor in the area to announce a contest: decorators could design and build an apartment

READY TO TALK TO GIRLS
WORKING THE STREETS

for each trafficked girl we rescued. Actually, each one is a two-room suite. The renovated suites would be judged by people who came to an open house, and the prize for the winner was an advertising spread in *Arizona Foothills Magazine*. Brian and Skye pursued the task wholeheartedly. Decorators spent from $50,000 to $100,000 on each suite, and they're spectacular. They used exotic woods, marble, and the finest furnishings. Today if you tour the apartments on the fourth floor of our Dream Center, you'll want to move in. The contractors poured thousands of dollars into each room, and one even used expensive, imported wood for the floor.

When the police bring us a girl they've rescued, she steps into the elevator frightened, confused, and often angry. But after we walk her down the fourth-floor hall and open the door to her residence for the next year, it's the finest home she's ever had.

LOVE FOR ALL AGES

Eventually, we ran out of room and opened another campus across town that ministers to forty-eight girls eleven to seventeen years old who had been trapped in trafficking. We named it Streetlight Ministries, and it's run by Brian's wife, Skye.

Sadly, not all the young girls turn the corner and leave the life of sex slavery. This was the case with Katie Lee, a fourteen-year-old girl who had developed a kidney failure from the intravenous drugs her captors forced her to use. As she got sicker and sicker, Skye often spent nights with her in the hospital. One night, Skye brought home a note that Katie Lee had written to Brian. As he read this little girl's words thanking him for all he had done for her, he suddenly realized it was her farewell. She was about to die in a bleak, sterile county hospital. After her passing, he began raising funds for an on-site medical center. Thanks to a major gift, the Phoenix Dream Center now has a state-of-the-art clinic to help keep our residents healthy.

As the reputation of our Dream Center in Phoenix spread, Brian got a call from the FBI. They had just shut down a polygamist compound in Colorado City, Utah, and asked if we could take some of the young girls who had the same father, Warren Jeffs. Brian and his team agreed to help, and soon the FBI brought a van full of girls dressed in clothes straight out of *Little House on the Prairie*. The girls were eager to change into the new clothes we provided for them.

Brian got another phone call, this time from the sixty-fifth "wife" of Warren Jeffs (he had a total of eighty-five). She said she had a house that she wanted to give to the Dream Center if we wanted it. Brian drove to Colorado City and discovered it wasn't just a house; it was the entire compound where Jeffs kept his eighty-five wives. It now serves as another Dream Center dedicated to restoring girls caught in sex trafficking.

Around this time, authorities began bringing young native American children to the Phoenix Dream Center, and that led to yet another campus—the Dream Center in Gallup, New Mexico. More than 500 people die each year in Gallup, mostly due to the effects of alcohol. According to law enforcement statistics, ninety-eight percent of America's cities are safer than Gallup. At the new Dream Center, we did what we do best: helping the people nobody else wants.

Brian can relate to these girls. He ran away from home when he was thirteen and began using drugs. By the time he was fourteen, he was homeless and sleeping in the alleys of Phoenix. He surrendered his life to Christ, went to college, and now leads one of the most in-novative Dream Centers in the world. And Skye? In addition to being fiercely dedicated to rescuing young girls from trafficking, she also happens to be the great-niece of Jackie Robinson, the famous baseball player who broke the color barrier in the sport.

Isn't it amazing what can happen when God puts a dream in some-one's heart? God has put ideas and directions on my heart countless times. When we want His will more than our own, we open the door to incredible possibilities. But how do we know an idea is God's will?

NO ONE IS LEFT OUT

His plans aren't always revealed in big, elaborate visions laid out in front of us. Often, He puts the seed of an idea in our minds, and we can either cultivate it or ignore it. In my opinion, the way to determine if those ideas come from God is to see if there's a need behind them. If you see a need, God is probably saying, "Go for it!" If there's any secret to the success God has given me, it's just that. Find a need and fill it; find a hurt and heal it. If you do that, you'll be squarely in the middle of God's will.

My passion for ministry came from watching my dad reach out to hurting people. From my earliest years, I learned that God loves everyone, but He has a special place in His heart for the poor and the hurting. In those first years, some critics accused me of "surface evangelism," or of playing the "numbers game." That's never really bothered me. I honestly believe leading people to faith in Christ is the best thing I can do for them. Each individual who comes forward

ASKING GOD TO BLESS

during an altar call is a person who needs Jesus—and whose life is far better with Jesus than without Him.

That's the center of all my dreams: people who need the Lord. That's the driving purpose that motivates me to keep doing what I'm doing. I spend most of my time traveling around the world encouraging others to dream big dreams for God and raising funds for people who are serving the forgotten and disadvantaged. I enjoy seeing how some of my dreams have influenced others to do things for the Lord that I could never do. God continues to surprise me with the opportunities.

Let me take a moment to share my perspective about the current state of the church. As I've talked to pastors from around the country, I'm afraid a lot of churches today fit Paul's description in 1 Corinthians 13 of being clanging cymbals because they aren't expressing the love of Jesus very well at all. These churches often major on doctrine but forget to demonstrate genuine care. We're not called to defend God

. . . or Christianity. That's not our job. Our God-given task is to show compassion (see Romans 12:9–13). Too often, we put limits on love: we want to help only "the deserving poor" who are victims of disasters, violence, and illness. The truth is that none of us deserved God's grace, yet He has lavished it on us! A tender, grace-changed heart isn't distracted or lazy; in other words, don't get lazy and sit on your purpose! In the passage in Romans, Paul also tells us to practice hospitality. *The Message* paraphrase says to "be inventive" in finding new ways to make people feel at home. Genuine love can be faked, but not for long. Sooner or later, the real motives of the heart are revealed. When we experience the love of Jesus, we'll look for ways to find a need and fill it, find a hurt and heal it. It's what Jesus did, and it's what His followers still do. That's my commitment, and I'm sure it's yours, too, or you wouldn't have read this far in the book!

In the early 90s, I was asked to preach at the National Black Pastors Conference in Washington, D.C. The invitation surprised me, so I asked the head of the organization, "Why did you invite me?"

"Because you have a black heart," he answered. What a great compliment! At the same time, I felt he had just set me up for a colossal failure because black preachers are some of the finest in the world. I was sure I couldn't possibly measure up.

I went to the event and preached my heart out. You haven't preached until you've preached to an auditorium filled with black preachers. My soul was energized by the shouts of "Amen!" and "Preach it, brother!" I didn't know, however, there was a young preacher in the audience who was about to give up. He pastored a little church that was struggling, and he needed a fresh touch from God or he was through. The title of my message was "A Miracle in the House." I told the audience of preachers that everything they needed to grow a great church was right there in the house: the intelligence, the creativity, the strategy, the seed money, and the faith . . . it was already there. And I issued this challenge: "Who is going to be the miracle in this house? Is it you?" I believed every word I uttered. God wants to perform incredible things, and He's given us all we need through the power of His Holy Spirit. But we have to step forward in faith and follow the dream He's placed in our hearts.

The young preacher got excited. In fact, he thought he was having a heart attack! He left the conference with one thought: *I'm going to be the miracle in the house*. He returned to his congregation of a few hundred people, and it began to grow. In fact, it grew so large that he was invited to preach on TBN. His message stirred the nation. After a couple of years, he decided to host his own pastors conference and invited me to speak. When he introduced me, he said, "After this man challenged me to be the miracle in the house, I decided that if I ever had my own pastors conference, I wanted him to be the opening speaker."

This preacher's name is T.D. Jakes. He was the miracle in the house that night!

The message I preached in that sermon is still true today. God has the power to perform any miracle He wants, but for some reason, He's chosen to do most of them through ordinary people like you and me. He could wave His arm and thousands would be saved, but He has given each of us the mission to reach the lost for Him. We are His ambassadors. He could pick up every little girl trapped in trafficking and cure every man or woman hooked on alcohol or drugs, but He calls us to be His hands, His arms, and His feet to care for them.

Decades ago, God gave me a vision and a promise. He put it in my heart to build a great church in Los Angeles and great churches around the world. I had no idea how He could accomplish something so big, but He has done it. Dream Centers are multiplying in cities in many countries, reaching people who probably would never come to church, and our Pastors & Leaders Schools have trained and encouraged 250,000 pastors to "excel still more." Time after time, God has astounded me with His leading, His love, His power, and His glory . . . and I'm immensely grateful.

As I approach the finish line, I don't think a lot about heaven. I can't wait to see Jesus face to face, but I'm willing to keep serving Him before I get to see Him. I'm sure it will be wonderful, but I love what I'm doing here on earth, and I plan to keep doing it until I take my last breath. This book is all about a great and mighty God who is able to use a flawed but willing man to bring glory to the name of Jesus. I didn't have all the answers and still don't, but I knew that God called me to reach people with the gospel, and His Holy Spirit took care of the rest. If He can use someone like me to do that, imagine what He can do through you.

And so, I leave you with this challenge. What are *you* doing? What dream do you have that's so big it will fail unless you trust in the power of God to fulfill it? What need do you see that simply must be met? What hurt are you aware of that needs to be healed?

There's still so much to be done: more people who are lost and need the Savior, more people who need the power of the Holy Spirit, more broken people who need to be healed, more hungry people who need to be fed, more prisoners who need encouragement and hope. Look around you and start dreaming. Maybe God wants you to be a friend to the friendless, to make sandwiches and give them to the people who live on the street, or maybe He wants you to open your home to a foster child, or volunteer to start a bus ministry at your church. He might even be asking you to start a Dream Center in your city, or volunteer at one in Brazil.

If you say "yes" to the dream God has placed on your heart, He'll give you everything you need to see it come true, and in the process, He'll make your life an adventure you never thought was possible.

Are you ready to dream big?

CHANGING MINDS, TOUCHING HEARTS

"You Can Do More!"

*A*s I reflect on the opportunities God has given me, three events stand out. The first happened when Johnny Cash and his touring group helped us pull off the world's biggest Sunday school. It was awesome, and after it was all over, I was euphoric. I couldn't believe we actually filled a baseball stadium with 30,000 people where so many people invited Jesus into their hearts for the first time.

As I left the stadium and headed for my car, a little guy approached me and said, "Pastor Barnett, that was amazing! Who would have thought that Johnny Cash would come to Davenport and bring his whole crew of musicians and sound technicians with him? Those 30,000 people packed into the stadium put you in the record books for the biggest Sunday school rally in the world. Best of all, 6,000 people accepted Jesus as their Savior!"

Then he looked up at me and pointed his finger in my face and said something that shocked me, "But you can do more."

PREACHING AT AN OUTDOOR RALLY

The second life-changing event occurred when we moved into our beautiful new church in Phoenix. I was worried that the move across town would hurt our attendance, but they came and I preached to a standing-room-only audience. What a great day! It was amazing to experience the glory of God that day.

After the service, I was practically walking on air as I made my way across the empty parking lot toward my car. At that moment, the little guy showed up again. "Oh, Pastor Barnett, wasn't that a great service? Remember when you thought building an auditorium that seated 6,500 was a real stretch? And now, on your first day in this wonderful new facility, it was filled to capacity. And to think that God gave you the message at the last minute. You must be so thrilled with what just happened!"

I was. We'd gone through tremendous growing pains to have a building big enough to accommodate our growth. I just smiled and breathed a prayer of thanks to God. Then the little guy looked me

DEBT-FREE LOS ANGELES DREAM CENTER

straight in the eye again and pointed his finger in my face just like he did in Davenport. "But, Pastor, you can do more."

The third significant event in my ministry happened when we finally paid off the debt on our first Dream Center. Years before, when Matthew initially brought up the idea of buying a run-down hospital, I didn't think it was possible. We had no money, and even if we did, we had no experience operating such an expansive facility to minister to the overwhelming needs of the poor, the homeless, the addicted, and the trafficked in Los Angeles. I'll never forget the day we burned the mortgage. Owning the building free and clear was clearly a miracle, and as I left to drive to the airport, guess who showed up again in the parking lot?

"Pastor," the little guy began. "You've really outdone yourself on this one. You faced many hurdles in buying this hospital and transforming it into a beacon of hope for all of Los Angeles to see what God can do. No one would have blamed you for walking away from it when it looked like you wouldn't be able to come up with the money to finish the restoration and pay it off, but God really came through, didn't He?"

I'll say! I have to admit it: that one was a real stretch. A huge risk. But the little guy was right: God really came through. As I paused for a moment to take it all in, the little guy continued. "But, Pastor," he said, as he pointed his finger in my face one more time, "you can do more."

It seems that every time God does something great in my life, that little guy shows up. I have no idea who he is. Sometimes I wonder if he even exists at all. Maybe he's a figment of my imagination, or maybe he's an angel. Maybe he's God's messenger to keep me from becoming complacent or satisfied. I don't know. But here's what I know for sure: in the time God allows me to continue to serve Him, I want to be that little guy for you.

I believe God wants to accomplish great things for His kingdom through you . . . if you'll only listen to Him and follow the dream He puts in your heart. No matter how big or small, if it's from God, He'll provide a way for you to realize your dream. And when you do, I want to be that little guy who points his finger in your face and says, "You can do even more!"

Because you can—not in your strength but through the power of God's Holy Spirit. Believe it! When you pray, lay your dreams in front of the One who is infinitely loving and powerful, and ask Him, "What if?"

This is my prayer for you:

Now to him who is able to do immeasurably more than all we ask or imagine, according to his power that is at work within us, to him be glory in the church and in Christ Jesus throughout all generations, for ever and ever! Amen. (Ephesians 3:20–21)

WHAT IF?

Acknowledgments

Marja – Without your prayers, support, and love, there wouldn't be a story. This is truly your story along with mine.

Dr. Kent Ingle – You and Southeastern University commissioned this book on my 80th birthday. I wouldn't have had the audacity to tell my story without your urging.

Chris Hodges – You are one of the greatest leaders in the body of Christ and one of my dearest friends. You have encouraged me beyond measure. I sure love you!

Dino Rizzo – You share my heart for the hurting and the poor. You and ARC have honored me by publishing this book. I respect you, admire you, and love you.

Joyce and Dave Meyer – Thank you for so graciously inviting me into your circle of love. Your authentic life of integrity has been a profound influence in my life. I value your friendship and love you so much!

Lynn Lane and Gary Blair – You have spent hours pulling together all the information and pictures needed to produce this book, which is a labor of love.

Steve and Susan Blount and Pat Springle – You were never satisfied with just acceptable. You wanted perfection. I appreciate you.

Jentezen Franklin – You are a truly great man and friend. You have loved and supported the dream beyond words. I so love you, thank you, and admire you.

Dr. George O. Wood – You are the man who challenged me to follow my dream and go to Los Angeles. Without your urging I probably would have never gone to LA. Thank you for enriching my life!

All of the pastors and churches who support the Dream Center – You are the heroes who made this miracle possible.

The ARC team and ARC churches – I appreciate the opportunity to partner with you to create more Dream Centers. I look forward to seeing how God will use you to change lives for generations to come.

"Where there is no Vision, the people perish."
Proverbs 19:18 KJV

"Where there are no people, the Vision perishes."
Tommy Barnett

To my GREAT GOD – who forgave me in my failures but never failed me.

"Just as I Am"

This hymn, often used for invitations to trust in Jesus, was written by Charlotte Elliott in 1835. Her biographer described the events that prompted her to write it. Her brother, a pastor, planned a bazaar to raise money to educate people who couldn't afford school. Biographer Frank Wallace explains:

The night before the bazaar she was kept wakeful by distressing thoughts of her apparent uselessness; and these thoughts passed by a transition easy to imagine into a spiritual conflict, till she questioned the reality of her whole spiritual life, and wondered whether it was anything better after all than an illusion of the emotions, an illusion ready to be sorrowfully dispelled. The next day, the busy day of the bazaar, she lay upon her sofa in that most pleasant boudoir set apart for her in Westfield Lodge, ever a dear resort to her friends. The troubles of the night came back upon her with such force that she felt they must be met and conquered in the grace of God. She gathered up in her soul the great certainties, not of her emotions, but of her salvation: her Lord, His power, His promise. And taking pen and paper from the table she deliberately set down in writing, for her own comfort, "the formulae of her faith." Hers was a heart which always tended to express its depths in verse. So in verse, she restated to herself the Gospel of pardon, peace, and heaven. "Probably without difficulty or long pause," she wrote the hymn, getting comfort by thus definitely "recollecting" the eternity of the Rock beneath her feet. There, then, always, not only for some past moment but "even now" she was accepted in the Beloved "Just as I am."[5]

1   Just as I am, without one plea,
       But that Thy blood was shed for me,
       And that Thou bid'st me come to Thee,
       O Lamb of God, I come! I come!

2   Just as I am, and waiting not
       To rid my soul of one dark blot;
       To Thee whose blood can cleanse each spot,
       O Lamb of God, I come, I come!

3   Just as I am, though tossed about
       With many a conflict, many a doubt;
       Fightings within, and fears without,
       O Lamb of God, I come, I come!

4   Just as I am, poor, wretched, blind;
       Sight, riches, healing of the mind;
       Yes, all I need, in Thee to find,
       O Lamb of God, I come, I come!

5   Just as I am, Thou wilt receive,
       Wilt welcome, pardon, cleanse, relieve;
       Because Thy promise I believe,
       O Lamb of God, I come, I come!

6   Just as I am, Thy love unknown
       Has broken every barrier down;
       Now, to be Thine, yea, Thine alone,
       O Lamb of God, I come, I come!

---

5   Frank Wallace, Spiritual Songsters (Chapter Two, 2000).

About the Author

Some have said that Tommy Barnett's greatest accomplishments are his children. As you've discovered by reading this book, Luke serves as the Senior Pastor at Dream City Church in Phoenix, Matthew is the Pastor of the Los Angeles Dream Center, and Kristie invests her life in her family and into the lives of women around the world. All three have the best of their dad's qualities of leadership, vision, creativity, compassion, and a passion to reach people with the gospel of Christ. And they all have their mother's charm and warmth, as well as her heart for hurting people.

This book tells the story of Tommy's life and legacy. Nothing more needs to be written about the ways God has used him to build great churches and organizations. What continues to be written are the countless ways other ministries learn from Tommy's heart and vision.

He serves on the board and executive committees of many evangelical organizations, including:

- Dream City Church, Phoenix, Arizona
- Phoenix Dream Center
- Los Angeles Dream Center
- New York Dream Center
- Joyce Meyer Ministries, Fenton, Missouri
- James Robison, Life Outreach International Ministry, Ft. Worth, Texas
- Ministries Today Magazine, Strang Communications, Lake Mary, Florida
- James Dobson, Focus on the Family, Pastoral Ministries Department, Colorado Springs, Colorado
- Dr. David Yonggi Cho, Church Growth International, Board of Directors, Seoul, Korea
- Chancellor of Southeastern University, Lakeland, Florida
- Former Chancellor of Grand Canyon University, Phoenix, Arizona

In addition, Tommy has received numerous awards, including:

- Honorary Doctor of Divinity Degree from Oral Roberts University, Tulsa, Oklahoma
- Honorary Doctor of Humane Letters Degree from Southern California Theological Seminary, Stanton, California
- Honorary Doctor of Divinity Degree from Southwestern Assembly of God University, Waxahachie, Texas
- 1999 Brotherhood of Man Award from the Religious Heritage of America Foundation

- 2011 Lifetime Achievement Award, Assemblies of God, Springfield, Missouri
- 2013 Lifetime Service Award, Southeastern University, Lakeland, Florida
- 2014 Nathaniel H. Bronner Vanguard Award, Austell, Georgia

Association of Related Churches

We are a global family of church and business leaders that exists to see a thriving church in every community reaching people with the message of Jesus. We provide relationships, resources, and opportunities to leaders of new and existing churches so that they can thrive.

WE LAUNCH

If you have a dream in your heart to start a life-giving church, ARC will come alongside you in the journey. ARC will provide resources, training, and coaching, to help you launch and grow a thriving church. The ARC launch model has been proven through the launch of hundreds of churches.

WE CONNECT

We don't want anyone to do ministry alone. ARC provides opportunities to connect with other pastors, church planters, and leadership mentors who have walked or are walking that same path as you. These relationships will support and strengthen you in what God has called you to do.

WE EQUIP

There are tremendous resources to draw from throughout the ARC Family. ARC continually creates and curates a wealth of teaching relating to life and ministry. We aim to cater these resources to the context and the needs of your local church.

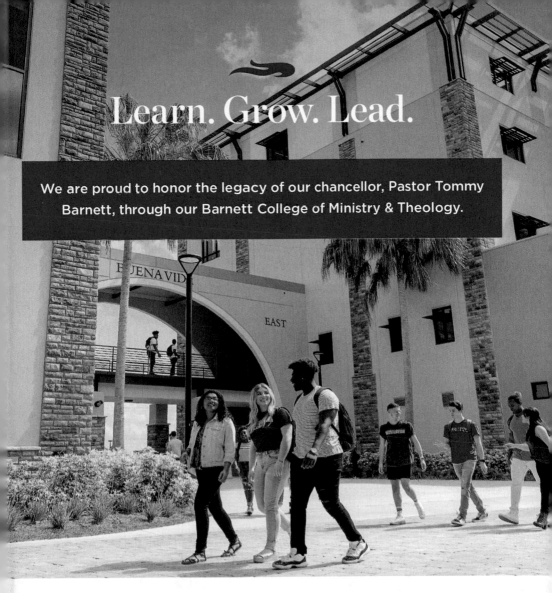

Learn. Grow. Lead.

We are proud to honor the legacy of our chancellor, Pastor Tommy Barnett, through our Barnett College of Ministry & Theology.

SOUTHEASTERN UNIVERSITY

OUR CONVENIENT, FLEXIBLE DEGREE FORMATS FIT YOUR LIFE

SEU offers affordable education online, at extension sites throughout the country, and at our main campus in Lakeland, Florida. Fields of study include ministry & theology, business & leadership, behavioral & social sciences, arts & media, natural & health sciences, and education & kinesiology.

SEU.edu/Barnett Lakeland, Florida
800.500.8760 | 863.667.5018

 **NETWORK**

WANT TO **MAKE A DIFFERENCE** IN YOUR CITY BUT DON'T KNOW WHERE TO START?

JOIN THE DREAM CENTER NETWORK

ALONGSIDE MORE THAN **300** OTHER DREAM CENTERS!

TO FIND OUT HOW, CONTACT **DCNETWORK@DREAMCENTER.ORG**

Resources

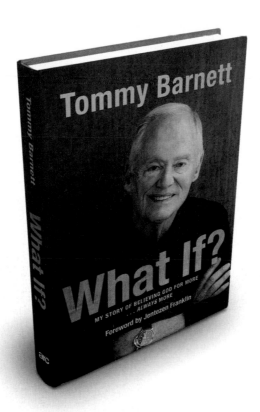

To purchase more copies of this book and to find out how
to obtain Pastor Tommy's many other books, go to

TommyBarnett.com

Not only do we want to come alongside pastors and leaders relationally, but we also believe in helping equip churches. The ARC Resources "How-To" series books are designed to give you practical tools and teaching from those who have proven that the methods help deliver the message of Jesus.